THE ENLIGHTENMENT PROCESS

JUDITH BLACKSTONE developed Subtle Self Work, a method of realizing fundamental consciousness, which she teaches in workshops throughout the United States and at Esalen Institute in Big Sur, California. She is also a psychotherapist and a dancer. She is author of *The Subtle Self: Personal Growth and Spiritual Practice.* For further information on Subtle Self Work, write to Realization Center, P.O. Box 1209, Woodstock, NY 12498.

THE ENLIGHTENMENT PROCESS

How It Deepens Your Experience
of Self, Body, and Community

Judith Blackstone

E L E M E N T

Rockport, Massachusetts • Shaftesbury, Dorset
Melbourne, Victoria

First published in the USA in 1997 by
Element Books, Inc.
PO Box 830, Rockport, MA 01966

Published in Great Britain in 1997 by
Element Books Limited
Shaftesbury, Dorset SP7 8BP

Published in Australia in 1997 by
Element Books Limited
and distributed by Penguin Books Australia Limited
487 Maroondah Highway, Ringwood, Victoria 3134

Text design/composition by Paperwork
Cover design by Slatter-Anderson, London
Printed in the USA by Courier Westford

Library of Congress Cataloging-in-Publication Data

Blackstone, Judith. 1947–
        The enlightenment process : how it deepens your experience of
self, body, and community / Judith Blackstone.
        p.   cm.
    Includes bibliographical references (p. i) and indexes.
    ISBN: 1-86204-059-1 (pbk. : alk. paper)
    1. Spiritual life.   2. Self-realization.   3. Spiritual exercises.
I. Title.
BL624.B524 1997   97-1882
291.4'24--dc21   CIP

British Library Cataloguing in Publication data available.

First Edition

ISBN   1-86204-059-1

10 9 8 7 6 5 4 3 2 1

Contents

Introduction

ONE OF THE MOST crucial and interesting debates in the personal growth field today is the question of whether or not the self exists. Most psychologists agree that a fully individuated self is the goal of human maturity but they differ widely in their description of the individuated or "whole" self. Many spiritual teachers claim that the sense of self is delusory and that the belief in the self is the greatest obstacle to spiritual progress. For contemporary seekers, who for the most part are pragmatic and nonsectarian and just want to "get on with it," this conflict of ideas is often a source of doubt and confusion. They ask: If I am to be more aware of my feelings and needs, if I am to think for myself and maintain my boundaries, how am I to achieve the cosmic unity and unconditional love promised in spiritual teachings? Am I supposed to feel that I don't exist? And if I am not truly a separate self, how should I reconcile myself to living in this separate shape? If the experience of my body is also delusory, how should I regard the sensations and hungers associated with the body?

This book is about the relationship between the sense of self and the unity of self and cosmos experienced in spiritual transcendence. Most writers on this subject have said that the self must first be developed in a psychological phase of growth and then somehow dismantled and transcended in a spiritual phase. I believe that this formulation reflects a misunderstanding of both the experience of authentic selfhood and the experience of spiritual transcendence.

The primary message of this book is that individuation and transcendence occur simultaneously, rather than sequentially. Although it seems paradoxical in theory, the actual experience of personal maturity is at once a sense of truly existing in our own distinct form, and of being continuous, unified, with all other forms in the environment and cosmos. We have a felt sense of becoming more substantial and more permeable at the same time. In the following chapters I describe how our most fundamental dimension of consciousness is the basis of both our sense of self and our spiritual transcendence. Our sense of self and our experience of cosmic unity develop at the same time, in the same way, through the realization of fundamental consciousness.

I call this dimension *fundamental consciousness* but it has been called by many names in the spiritual literature of the world. The Buddhists call it emptiness or Buddha-nature, describing it as the pristine ground of life. The Hindus call it Brahman, describing it as pure, unconditioned consciousness. In the West it has been called Godhead, cosmic consciousness, and unity consciousness.

Fundamental consciousness is beyond our mental concepts, psychological projections, images, and archetypes. It is deeper than the physical and energetic levels of our being. Hindu metaphysics teaches that energy and physical matter are transformations of pure consciousness, so that our being and all other forms in nature are basically made of pure consciousness.

Fundamental consciousness is experienced as clear, open, unified space pervading our body and our environment, transcending the duality of self and object. Since fundamental consciousness is not a mental concept, and not an object of consciousness but consciousness itself, it is difficult to comprehend until one has experienced it. One image often used to convey the experience of fundamental consciousness is the mirror, because fundamental consciousness reflects everything it pervades, while remaining empty and unchanged itself. Fundamental consciousness is not transient like the inner and outer events it reflects. It holds steady like a mirror while each moment of sensation, emotion, thought, perception, and action occurs and vanishes in its reflection.

Fundamental consciousness pervades, and is the basis of, every cell in our body and every atom of the universe. Because it pervades our body, it is the basis of our individual wholeness. Because it pervades the universe, it is the basis of our oneness, our continuity, with all nature.

In Eastern traditions, the realization of fundamental consciousness is called enlightenment. Many people today are ready for enlightenment, and they are drawn to the profound Eastern teachings. But these teachings can reduce our spiritual path to an exotic labyrinth if we do not understand one essential fact: Enlightenment is a relative term. We begin with a partial attunement to fundamental consciousness, and very gradually our attunement deepens and expands. According to Eastern metaphysics the process of self-realization completes itself in the ultimate extinction of the individual self. We might assume from this that we become more extinct as we progress, but we would be wrong. For the long duration of our path towards complete enlightenment, we are becoming more of our individual self. We transcend our individual self while completing our self—by gradually attuning to fundamental consciousness throughout our entire form.

As I will explain, we realize fundamental consciousness by accessing the subtle channel in the vertical core of our body. The more access we have to this channel, the more realization we have of fundamental consciousness, pervading our body and our environment. Therefore individuation and transcendence both occur as a result of penetrating inward to the vertical core of the body. They are one and the same process.

As we access the vertical core and attune to the most fundamental dimension of our body, we bring to fruition the natural potentials of our being enfolded in our body, such as understanding, love, power, and sexuality. This gives us a sense of becoming whole. We experience our whole body at once, and we experience all the basic qualities of our being at once. We not only know *about* our self (our history, preferences, and so on), we know our self, we experience our own being. Until that far-off moment when we know our self completely, our experience of being will be contained around an integrative core that is our unique perspective, our unique location in the vast, unbounded space of fundamental consciousness. If we attempt to eradicate our sense of self, we thwart our spiritual progress and rob ourselves of the great joy of becoming whole. This book addresses a phase of personal growth that is usually ignored in both psychological and spiritual literature: the gradual deepening of enlightenment, following the initial realization of fundamental consciousness. In this phase we learn to live in the empty, pervasive space of fundamental consciousness, in union with the environment and cosmos, while becoming integrated, alive, and whole within the perimeters of our own body.

In order to describe the relationship between the sense of self and spiritual transcendence, it is important that these terms are clearly understood. In chapter 1, I define enlightenment and describe the experience of living in the dimension of fundamental consciousness. This is a radical shift from a fragmented perception of I and other to an experience of our inner and outer life occurring in a single, unbroken field of consciousness. Barriers between our self and our experience that we may not even have known were there, dissolve: We find ourselves in immediate, vivid contact with life.

Chapter 2 presents four different interpretations of the words self and selflessness that are often confused by spiritual students: the true or essential self, the false self, ethical selflessness, and ultimate

selflessness. I describe what it feels like to become an essential self
and how the qualities inherent in fundamental consciousness give us
our authentic sense of self.

Chapter 3 is about the relation of psychological healing to
enlightenment. The progression towards enlightenment is a natural,
spontaneous human growth process. The infant's budding sense of
I and other evolves naturally towards the mature individuation and
cosmic oneness of the spiritual master, or would evolve if it were
not for the inevitable binding of childhood pain in the body. In
this section I describe how psychological binding occurs, how it
impedes our realization of fundamental consciousness, and how
it can be released.

Chapter 4 is about the relation of self and other in the dimension
of fundamental consciousness. In our everyday interactions with
people, the shift from fragmentation to the oneness of enlightenment
is a shift in our sense of boundaries. On one level, boundaries are a
question of how much we give to others, how much we allow ourselves to receive from others, and what we consider intrusion or
abuse. But there is a more subtle level of boundaries that can be
described as the placement of our consciousness in relation to our
body and the bodies of other people. As I will explain, most people
create artificial boundaries to separate themselves from other people,
or they attempt to live without boundaries, losing contact with their
own body and self to connect with others. In fact, most of us manage
to do both.

When we become enlightened, we realize that our fundamental
dimension of consciousness is continuous with the fundamental consciousness of other people. There is no true barrier between us. At
the same time, we are beginning to live in the vertical core of our
body and to relate to the world from this innermost core. The shift
inward to our core is a deepening perspective on the world; it feels
as if we are relating to people from further away. There is a sense

that we are finding our true distance from other people as we discover our oneness with them. We are also beginning to experience our distinct shape in space, our individual wholeness. In the dimension of fundamental consciousness, we experience our own wholeness and our unity with other people at the same time. We experience the deepest possible connection, without any loss of our own self.

In chapter 5, I show how the realization of fundamental consciousness transforms the body as well as our experience of embodiment. Our sense of identity shifts from the muscular surface of our body to the fundamental dimension of pure, unified consciousness pervading our body. I describe how this shift effects our breath, the use of our senses, our physical comfort and health, and our relation to gravity.

Chapter 6 describes how our underlying oneness with the vast dimension of fundamental consciousness, pervading all of the cosmos, informs and guides our progress towards enlightenment. There is a constant dialogue between the incomplete self and the whole of cosmic fundamental consciousness, which can be consciously engaged in through communion with nature, meditation, visualization, and prayer. The mechanism of our personal growth is neither within the individual nor outside of the individual, but in the relationship between the individual and the cosmos.

One of my purposes in writing this book is to bring the notion of enlightenment out of the realm of fantasy and esoteric speculation. To be enlightened is to realize one's own nature as fundamental consciousness. Enlightenment is available to everyone—it is our birthright, the natural outcome of human maturation. Ultimate reality is just reality, clearly experienced. Once felt, it is unmistakable; we have an inherent ability to recognize reality. Enlightenment is not an abstraction or a fantasy, but our most concrete sense of truly existing, and our natural, normal kinship with all other people, animals, plants, oceans, mountains, planets, and stars.

The model of personal growth presented in this book is based on my own experience and on the experience of the many people whose growth I have been privileged to witness as a teacher and therapist. Although I have had many teachers, my understanding has been most influenced by the Performance Technique of Amos Gunsberg, the Zen teaching of John Daido Loori, and the non-dual Vedantic teaching of Sathya Sai Baba. The method of work described throughout the book is called Subtle Self Work. My last book, *The Subtle Self: Personal Growth and Spiritual Practice,* describes how I developed this work. The Subtle Self Work is a series of gentle, precise attunement exercises to help people realize their authentic self and their oneness with the cosmos in the dimension of fundamental consciousness.

I include exercises from the Subtle Self Work so that the reader may better understand the experience I am trying to describe. But this is not a self-help book. The full benefit of the exercises requires the guidance of a qualified Subtle Self Work teacher. I also describe the experiences of some of the people I have worked with as a Subtle Self Work teacher and psychotherapist. For the sake of their privacy, every one of these descriptions is a compound of several different people and events, and all names are fictitious.

My intention in this book is to bring some clarity to understanding the process of becoming enlightened. I present the individuation of the self, the transcendence of the self, the transformation of the body, and the deepening communion with other life as equally important, concurrent aspects of the realization of fundamental consciousness. I hope to convey both the preciousness and the accessibility of this realization.

1

Defining Enlightenment

Enlightenment Is a Specific Phase of Maturity

LIFE HAS MEANING because it has direction. It has a goal. Most of us create meaning in our lives by creating goals for ourselves, such as family, wealth, artistic achievement. But life has a goal that we don't have to create, that is inherent in its nature, in our nature. Our own personal life evolves towards a specific destination which is sometimes called self-realization, or enlightenment. Just as our created goals are based on our desire for something, we also have a fundamental desire for life's inherent goal. It is this underlying desire for enlightenment that often causes us to feel unfulfilled, even after we have achieved our created goals.

The word enlightenment is often used in a general way to describe a variety of experiences. But in Subtle Self Work, as in most Eastern religious teachings, enlightenment refers to a specific phase of human maturity, a specific and unmistakable shift in the way one experiences life. Although enlightenment is the most concrete actual experience of being alive, to describe it always sounds abstract, until you have experienced it yourself. For this reason I have included exercises from Subtle Self Work to help you experience the dimension of consciousness that I am attempting to describe.

To understand the relationship of enlightenment and self, and how they both mature at the same time, we need to clearly understand the specific experiences that are meant by the words enlightenment and self. The following definitions of enlightenment are based on my own experience, the experience of friends and students, and on the definitions found in the spiritual texts of Buddhism and Hinduism. The point I wish to emphasize is that the definitions offered here are not solely from my subjective experience (for then they could be fantasy) and are also not solely the paraphrasing of long-dead sages from old books (for they might be naive or metaphorical). Rather they are descriptions that many people agree on, based on their own experience, that support the validity of the ancient texts.

Enlightenment Is the Realization of Fundamental Consciousness

Enlightenment is the realization, the lived experience, that we are made of pure consciousness, that pure consciousness is our fundamental nature and our ultimate reality. And that everything else in the universe is also made of pure consciousness, so that our own being is fundamentally unified with all of nature. As one fourth-century Chinese sage put it, "Everything in the universe is of one and the same root as my own self." In enlightenment, we experience life from the vantage point of that root.

We experience our own self as unbroken consciousness, pervading our body and our environment. This means that there is a continuity between our inner and outer perception. We have a sense of vast space, as if all our perceptions were one single tapestry of reflections in a single mirror. We feel that we are made of clear, empty space, finer than air, unbounded, and motionless. Within this vast space moves the changing progression of our thoughts, feelings, sensations, and perceptions.

In Subtle Self Work I call this unbroken, pervasive dimension fundamental consciousness. Before we realize fundamental consciousness we identify our self as our sensations, feelings, perceptions, ideas, memories. But when we realize fundamental consciousness, we recognize that these discrete, transitory experiences come and go within the fundamental ground that is our true identity.

When people begin to realize fundamental consciousness, they report that they feel translucent, or permeable. One man told me excitedly that he had discovered that the world was round, because he could now experience the space behind him, and to the sides of him, rather than just in front of him. As I will describe throughout this book, the shift from our frontal self-object relationship with the world to an experience of continuity with the world affects every aspect of our life, including our ability to understand and to love, even our physical health. A woman told me that before realization, she felt that she was watching life; now she felt she was participating. Experiencing a continuity with the world, she felt a basic kinship with everything she encountered. And because she experienced her inner responses at the same time as she experienced the outer world, she felt engaged in the encounters.

Enlightenment Is Becoming Real

Consciousness is our ultimate reality. In Hindu metaphysics ultimate reality is called *Brahman* in Sanskrit and is described like this: "I am the supreme Brahman which is pure consciousness, always clearly manifest, unborn, one only, imperishable, unattached and all-pervading and non-dual." Although this description, from the ninth century Indian philosopher Shankara, may sound exotic or abstract, every word is soberly meant as a description of the fundamental reality of every human being. Reality is the opposite of the abstract. It is real.

In enlightenment, we experience that we are becoming real—not something new, but something we have always been but only barely known. This is what Shankara means by unborn: The unified, pervasive pure consciousness has always been there, pervading our every cell. It is the true, whole "I" that is our inherent, fundamental nature, hidden behind the partial, fragmented, abstract "I"s that we tolerate before we know of our wholeness. We do not have to create reality; it has always been there. But the ability to recognize reality is also inherent in us. All our life we have been guided by our ability to tell truth from deception, balance from disharmony. As we realize fundamental consciousness we recognize that our underlying reality has been the goal of our life-long navigation and desire.

Enlightenment is an experience unlike any other we have had because there is no duality in it. We do not have an experience *of* fundamental consciousness. Although the limits of language make it necessary for us to use the preposition of, fundamental consciousness is actually realizing itself. It is self-reflecting. The knower and the known are the same. Fundamental consciousness is our own ordinary consciousness, but directly, purely experienced, without the usual "veils" of habit, confusion, and defense. Enlightenment is the phase of human maturity in which the mind comes to know itself.

The state of continuity within our self and between our self and our environment is our inherent, and actually most normal state. Several people have expressed fear to me about who they will become if they allow themselves to become enlightened. But once they have realized fundamental consciousness, they see that they have only become themselves, a deeply familiar and instantly recognizable being.

Some Misconceptions about Enlightenment

Enlightenment is much easier to experience than most people think. I've watched people stomp angrily out of workshops because I was asking them to experience what the revered masters have experienced, as if the attempt were futile and even sacrilegious. I want to emphasize, as I said in the introduction, that enlightenment is a relative term. A Zen master once told me, "Enlightenment is easy to achieve. But to realize it completely can take many lifetimes." In this way it is something like being pregnant. You can be a little bit pregnant and no one would say that you are not "really" pregnant, but you have not yet come to full term. There is a tremendous range between the advanced enlightenment of the masters and the bit of enlightenment of which we are all capable. When we first become enlightened, we have begun a phase of maturity that potentially stretches far ahead of us. But the beginning of enlightenment, as well as its progressive deepening, is accessible to anyone who is interested in it.

There is also a tendency for us to impose the sense of sanctity that some of us were taught in the Judeo-Christian tradition onto these principles of enlightenment. Much of Western religion teaches an attitude of reverence and humility towards a distant god, an image of patriarchal authority that we can petition but never truly know. Religious students are treated as children who can sit in the protective, vigilant presence of God, but who have only the responsibility of obedience. In the more ritualistic forms of Eastern religion as well, there is a hushed, hallowed quality when discussing the ultimate, and certainly there is great respect shown for the spiritual masters.

But the more advanced the teaching, and the students, become, the more the ultimate is presented as something belonging to us, as a wonderful but entirely usual part of our own nature, that can be neither taken away nor given to us by any external presence. I have found that many people who are ready for enlightenment are not achieving it because they assume it is some far-distant exalted state. The work that so many of us have been doing to become more real, more open to life, has been leading towards the realization of our fundamental dimension of consciousness. It is crucial to our personal growth that we recognize our essential reality and demystify our understanding of enlightenment.

Another related misconception about enlightenment is that it is an "altered" state of consciousness. Enlightenment is often confused with the peak experiences that many people have, for example, while looking up at the stars, or witnessing the birth of a baby. But a peak experience is by definition a momentary event, often accompanied by intense emotions such as awe or ecstasy. Enlightenment is not a momentary alteration of consciousness that one goes to and returns from. For this same reason it also differs from the state of being hypnotized, and the trance state. Enlightenment is a clear, alert perception of the present moment that represents a lasting refinement of consciousness.

Some people do have their first entry into enlightenment as a peak experience, a *satori*, in which they are dazzled by the sudden shift into the unity of fundamental consciousness. And some have had sudden deepenings of enlightenment as well, in which they abruptly experience much more of the space of fundamental consciousness than before. But enlightenment itself is not a temporary, nor a particularly charged, emotional state. It is a lasting transformation of our being, involving our ongoing relation to our self and our environment.

Sometimes enlightenment is said to be instantaneous because there is a definitive difference between being in the dimension of fundamental consciousness, and not being in it. Some people notice this difference suddenly, while others, once they do notice it, feel that they have been there for a while without registering or naming it. One may lose the realization of fundamental consciousness and get it back several times before it becomes stable. But once we do become stable in our realization, we continue to live there, while our realization very gradually deepens and expands. This means that our experience of fundamental consciousness gradually pervades more of our body, increasing our sense of inner depth and wholeness, and opening new realms of sensitivity and insight. And it gradually increases our sense of oneness with other people, with nature, and with the cosmos. The most advanced spiritual masters, those rare few who are completely, or almost completely, enlightened, are said to be omniscient and omnipresent. They have realized the entire ground of fundamental consciousness, pervading the whole universe.

One point that sometimes causes confusion about the gradual, relative nature of enlightenment is that Buddhist teachers make a distinction between what they call the gradual or progressive path and the direct or sudden path. These terms refer to the methods used to attain the initial realization of fundamental consciousness, and not to the subsequent process of deepening one's realization. The method offered in Subtle Self Work is a direct path because it aims to evoke an immediate experience of fundamental consciousness. Gradual paths work with ritual and visualization techniques, cultivating concentration, dedication, discipline, and virtuous behavior as preparatory conditions for enlightenment. A direct path aims to evoke an immediate experience of fundamental consciousness. But a direct or sudden path does not mean that we become completely enlightened all at once.

Sometimes the question is asked why we have to work to achieve the realization of a dimension that is naturally part of ourselves. The Buddha taught that we are already enlightened; we are just not aware of it. But why not? Zen Buddhism speaks of our "beginningless greed, anger, and ignorance" that separate us from the recognition of our true nature. Hinduism points to an accumulation over many lifetimes of confusion and attachments that pull us outward from our true self and obscure the basic purity of our consciousness. This explanation also puts the beginning of our trouble in the unfathomable past. And the Bible offers its own Rorschach-like allegory of our fall from grace in the garden. One thing is clear. We are not born enlightened. Children, although undefended, are not experiencing the whole of the dimension of fundamental consciousness. There is a vast difference between the openness and unguarded love of an infant and the far-reaching clarity and intense but detached love of a spiritual master. As adults we must grow towards enlightenment, as well as release the psychological defenses that impede this growth. Although there is much literature on what separates us from fundamental consciousness, why we must work to realize what has been there all along remains unanswered.

I believe that the most confused and potentially destructive misconception about enlightenment is the notion that the realization of fundamental consciousness is also the eradication of the sense of self. But that is the subject of the next chapter.

EXERCISE 1   *Attunement to Fundamental Consciousness*

Here is an exercise to help you experience the fundamental dimension of consciousness.

Sit upright on a chair or cross-legged on a pillow.

Close your eyes and focus on your breathing.

Now bring your attention down to your feet, and feel that you are inside your feet, that you inhabit your feet. Experience the inner volume of your feet.

Now the same with your ankles—experience that you are inside your ankles, filling them with yourself.

Feel that you are inside your lower legs.

Feel that you are inside your knees. Now balance your awareness of the inside of both knees. Find both those inner areas at exactly the same time.

Feel that you are inside your thighs.

Feel that you are inside your hip sockets. Balance your awareness of the inside of your hip sockets; find them both at the same time.

Feel that you are inside your pelvis. Let yourself feel the quality of your gender inside your pelvis. Experience that your breath moves through the quality of your gender, inside your pelvis.

Feel that you are inside your midsection, between your

pelvis and ribs. Feel the quality of your personal power inside your midsection. Experience that your breath moves through the quality of power, inside your midsection.

Feel that you are inside your chest. Feel the quality of your love, inside your chest. Experience that your breath moves through the quality of love, inside your chest.

Feel that you are inside your shoulders.

Feel that you are inside your shoulder sockets. Balance your awareness of the inside of your shoulder sockets; find them both at the same time.

Feel that you are inside your arms, wrists, and hands, inside each finger.

Feel that you are inside your neck. Feel the quality of your voice, your potential to speak, inside your neck. Experience that your breath moves through the quality of your voice, inside your neck.

Experience that you are inside your head—behind your forehead, inside your eyeballs, behind your cheekbones, and inside your jaw all the way to the hinges of your jaw. And inside your brain, inside both hemispheres of your brain. Feel the quality of your understanding, inside your whole brain. Experience that your breath moves through the quality of understanding, inside your brain.

Now feel that you are inside your whole body all at once. If we say that the body is the temple, then you are sitting inside the temple.

Keep your breath smooth and even, as you inhabit your whole body.

Keeping your eyes closed, mentally find the space outside your body, the space in the room.

Experience that the space inside your body and outside your body is the same continuous field of space. Let it pervade you. Let your breath be so fine that it moves through the space, on the inhale and the exhale, without disturbing the stillness of the space. Your body is still, the space pervading your body is still— only the breath is moving. The breath should feel like a mixture of breath and mind.

Now open your eyes.

With your eyes open, feel that you are inside your whole body at once.

Mentally find the space outside your body.

Experience that the space inside and outside your body is the same continuous field of space. It pervades you.

Experience that the space pervades your body and also pervades the objects around you, and pervades the other people in the room. Everything and everyone is pervaded by the same space, the same dimension of fundamental consciousness.

Experience that the space pervading your own body also pervades the walls of the room.

Let your breath be fine and even. The breath passes through the space of your body without disturbing it.

Be very patient with this exercise. Most people shift their mind slightly on each breath. Do not try to forcibly hold your mind still, but keep relaxing and settling into the stillness until you can breathe without disturbing it.

Now let yourself sit for a few minutes in the clear, pervasive space of fundamental consciousness. Breathe silently and smoothly. Let your thoughts, feelings and sensations occur in the field of fundamental consciousness without disturbing or changing it in any way.

Sometimes when I teach this exercise, people ask me how large they should visualize the space outside of them. This is not a visualization exercise. The space of fundamental consciousness is really there. We are only realizing it. The space will be as large as you are capable of realizing it at this time. If you do not immediately experience the space inside and outside your body as one unified space, you will after several attempts. The repeated intention to experience fundamental consciousness will finally evoke the new "wiring" needed for this subtle experience.

People also ask me what to do about distracting thoughts as they attune to fundamental consciousness. Our thoughts, feelings, sensations, and perceptions are the content of the clear space of fundamental consciousness. They do not affect fundamental consciousness. So you can let your thoughts, feelings, and sensations occur, while remaining in the realization of fundamental consciousness. If you find that you become so focused on your thoughts that you lose the experience of fundamental consciousness, simply bring yourself back to that experience. There is nothing "wrong" or "unspiritual" about having thoughts, emotions, or sensations. The advanced spiritual teachers are very clear that being enlightened does not mean having an unthinking mind, but rather a "non-abiding" mind, a mind that is not fixated on thoughts or feelings but allows them to occur unhindered. As you become stable in fundamental consciousness, all of the content of your consciousness will flow freely and vividly through you. The depth and clarity of our reception and response to life increases as we become enlightened because we are no longer trying to control or defend against our experience.

Enlightenment Is Unity

To become enlightened is to move from a fragmented experience of life to a unified experience. Before we become enlightened our focus shifts from self to object, or from one modality of experience to another. We may experience another person quite fully but be only barely aware of our self. In another moment we know our own feelings but our perception of the outside world is diminished. Or we may know our thoughts but not be conscious of our feelings, or sensations.

When we become enlightened we have realized the continuity —the unity—of inner and outer consciousness. Thus we feel a continuity, a wholeness, of inner and outer experience, without any shifting of focus. This means that there is no longer any divisive schism between subject and object, or between thought, feeling, and sensation. For example, at this moment, sitting at my computer, I am aware of the objects around me (their form and texture), including the window in front of my desk and the bit of earth and tree trunk that I can see while looking down at my work. This is my outer experience. At the same time, I am aware of the sensation of being in my body, the emotional content of the moment (even though there is no particular emotional charge at the moment there is still an emotional tone that is always present) and the intensity of my mental activity—my inner experience. All of these perceptions are a unified whole; they exist in a single unbounded space, and the space itself has a luminous, vibrant quality. I and other become one whole in the one pervasive field of fundamental consciousness. As I will explain in the next chapter and in chapter 4, this wholeness of I and other does not negate the integrity of the individual wholeness of each person or object. In fact, our individual boundaries are more defined in the dimension of fundamental consciousness. Once we can experience our own inner life at the same time as we experience the outer world, it becomes very clear where we leave off and the world begins.

Enlightenment Is Direct Experience

To become enlightened is to experience life directly, without the interference of psychological defenses, projections, and preconceptions, and without the distraction of our habitual mental chatter. As fundamental consciousness, we pervade both the subject and the object of experience, the perceiver and the perceived. We thus experience no barrier, no gap, between our self and our experience.

For example, a woman had worked with me for two years and

thoroughly explored her childhood history, releasing much of the pain of growing up in a chaotic, alcoholic family. One day Ruth came to the session in tears, saying that she had just realized that she had been seeing her life "through a filter." She said that she had suddenly caught a glimpse of herself in the mirror and realized that she had not been seeing herself as she really is. She had either superimposed an image of herself on the reflection in the mirror, based on a fashion magazine ideal, or she had seen herself as her feared, negative image of herself, misshapen and homely. She had been afraid to see herself directly, without the filter. She also realized that she was not seeing her husband clearly, or the other important people in her life. She was afraid that if she saw them directly, she would either see that they did not really love her, or she would see something that she did not like, and reject them. Yet she felt that much of her social awkwardness arose from the fact that she was not seeing people as they truly are, but rather idealizing or diminishing them.

This "filter" of Ruth's is actually typical of the human condition, but not many people ever notice the filter. As we realize fundamental consciousness, we see through the veils of our projections and defenses to experience life as it really is. There is a Zen story that addresses this same theme. A monk and his teacher are walking in the teacher's garden. The monk asks his teacher to explain the phrase that I have already quoted: "The whole universe is of one and the same root as my own self." The teacher points to a rose and says, "Most people see this flower as if they were in a dream." The dream the teacher refers to is the cloudiness of our consciousness that separates us from our direct experience of life.

When we are not enlightened, we live abstractly, in our idea of life. Instead of seeing this particular flower, we see a general flower, like an image from a file in our mind marked "flower." And our "flower file" may be full of memories and associations that cause us to respond to the flower with feelings that are not directly related to this particular flower. In other words, we respond in a distorted or diminished way to our distorted or diminished perception of the world.

Our abstract perception of the world is to some degree a fantasy, and whether it is a romance or a horror story, it is not as satisfying as the direct experience of life. When we realize fundamental consciousness, we begin to truly see, truly touch, truly hear. We move from abstraction to substance, from imagination to actuality.

Many people fear that the actual world will be dull and ugly, compared to their abstract dream-life. But our senses, when (relatively) unfettered by psychological defense and fantasy, reveal a more vivid, more balanced world than we ever imagined. If we are seeing a preconceived flower, a composite of many past flowers, we will not notice the richness of color, softness of texture, the exact form of the present flower, and we will certainly not see the subtle radiance that surrounds the flower, that matches the light of our own aliveness. We will not notice that the flower is pervaded by the same radiant emptiness that pervades our own body, that we are inseparably unified with the flower in the emptiness of pure consciousness that is the root of all things in the universe.

In enlightenment, our senses become unified. We experience life as a unified field of energy vibrating in a unified field of pure, empty consciousness. This vibration is registered by all of our senses at once. We have a single, unified impression of life that is seen, heard, touched (felt), smelled, tasted all at the same time. This adds fullness and resonance to all our experience. For example, when we perceive the aliveness inside a branch of a tree, in the dimension of fundamental consciousness we experience that we are "seeing-feeling-hearing" it. The poet Rainer Maria Rilke describes this unified perception when he thanks the mythic musician Orpheus for "creating a tree in the ear." Rilke's Orpheus is attuned to the subtle foundation of life in which the visible world is audible and the audible world is visible.

EXERCISE 2 *Seeing and Hearing with Fundamental*
Consciousness

Here are two variations on an exercise for direct experience.

2A) With your eyes closed, feel that you are inside your whole body at once. Now mentally find the space outside your body. And experience that the space outside and inside your body is the same continuous field of space pervading you.

Keeping your eyes closed, let yourself hear the sounds around you. Make no effort to listen to them, but just allow them to occur in the field of fundamental consciousness. Experience that the sounds occur in the space without changing or disturbing the space. The sounds are movement, patterns of vibration, occurring in the motionless space of fundamental consciousness.

Now open your eyes, and again find the space inside your body, outside your body, and inside and outside your body at the same time. Experience how the space that pervades your body also pervades the objects and the walls of the room.

With your eyes open, let yourself hear the sounds around you, without making any effort to listen to them. Now let yourself see whatever is in your field of vision, without any effort to look at it. Let the objects simply occur in your vision, as vibrational patterns in the field of fundamental consciousness. Experience that you are seeing with the field of consciousness, rather than with your eyes. The eyes are just lenses; your consciousness sees.

Now let yourself see and hear at the same time, without any effort. The field of consciousness is seeing and hearing.

You can also practice the visual exercise with a moving object, such as a flickering candle flame, steam rising from a pot, or the flight of birds. Keep relaxing your focus so that your field of vision remains absolutely still, while the visual stimulus moves through it. This can only be accomplished by relaxing your focus, not by forcibly holding your vision still.

Here is one more exercise for direct seeing.

2B)   Again find the space inside your body, outside your body, and both outside and inside at the same time, so that space is pervading you. Now choose an object in your field of vision and let yourself see it without any effort. Experience that the same space that pervades your body also pervades the object. Do not project your vision, or your consciousness, through the object, but just attune to the space that is already pervading the object. Again, it feels as if the field of consciousness itself is seeing the object—as if you and the object are both embedded in one perceptual field. Zen Buddhism describes this experience as "The man sees the mountain, the mountain sees the man."

Recently I was teaching this exercise in a beautiful country setting, overlooking the sea. One woman in the group expressed concern that the ocean would no longer look as beautiful if she did the exercise, because she would be looking through it rather than at it. She was making the common mistake of projecting her vision through the object, rather than relaxing her vision and seeing with fundamental consciousness. By the end of the week, she was amazed that the ocean looked more magnificent than she had ever seen it. She was experiencing it directly, without the filter of habit or defense. Fundamental consciousness pervades the object and reflects it back to us without distortion.

The eyes are one of the most defended parts of the body, for almost everyone. In Subtle Self Work, particular emphasis is put on relaxing the eyes and seeing with fundamental consciousness. If we do not relax our eyes, our way of looking at the world will keep us in the fragmented condition of I and other, rather than the unity, or continuity, of I and other that is experienced in fundamental consciousness. In order to live in this unified dimension, we need to allow the visual images around us to exist as they really are, without defending against them. To experience life directly, we need to receive the world, just as it is, in the empty, unobstructed field of fundamental consciousness.

Enlightenment Is the Realization of the Eternal

The dimension of fundamental consciousness never changes. When we realize this most subtle dimension of our self, we experience a vast, unchanging stillness pervading our body and our environment. We feel that we ourselves are fundamentally timeless and changeless. Zen Buddhism expresses this with the phrase, "I have never moved from the beginning."

Yet the life that occurs within our fundamental consciousness is all movement and change. All the "systems" that make up our being, such as our blood, nerve impulses, our stream of mental associations, our meridians of subtle energy, as well as the flow of circumstances in our lives, are in constant motion. The more we experience the absolute stillness of fundamental consciousness, the more freely and efficiently the movement of life takes place. We become healthier physically, we respond more deeply emotionally, and our thinking becomes clearer and more creative.

If you practice the exercise of attuning to fundamental consciousness (exercise 1), you may feel streamings of energy inside your body. Like fundamental consciousness, energy is an essential aspects of ourselves and the cosmos. The more open we are to life (the less defended we are psychologically), the more energy we feel in our body.

Although energy is an essential aspect of our nature for the duration of our growth towards wholeness, it is not our ultimate reality. Hindu metaphysics says that energy is a condensation or contraction of pure consciousness, and physical matter is a condensation of energy. It is the imbalance created by this mysterious contraction of pure consciousness that produces the dynamic flux, the myriad cycles, the creative chaos and sexy friction, the war and illness or vague discomfort that is our life on this planet. Hindu metaphysics also teaches that in complete enlightenment we accomplish a balance that is again pure consciousness, and we are no longer reborn in the world of energy and matter.

In our phenomenal world, pure consciousness pervades energy and physical matter, and energy pervades physical matter. Many people practicing spiritual and therapeutic disciplines reach the dimension of energy before they realize fundamental consciousness. The shift into the experience of oneself as energy from the experience of oneself as only physical matter, or only mental concepts, is so radical and liberating that many people assume they have reached the ultimate dimension of existence. It is important for our continuing maturity that we understand that fundamental consciousness is primary, and pervades the energy in our body and in the cosmos. The cultivation of energy without the realization of fundamental consciousness can exacerbate our imbalance and discomfort.

When we have a lot of energy in our body but have not yet realized fundamental consciousness, we often feel overwhelmed by our own energy and the energy in the environment. The realization of fundamental consciousness grounds us in our true sense of self, as I will explain more fully in the next chapter, and centers us in the vertical core of our body. If we experience our own nature as the clear, unchanging stillness of fundamental consciousness, our energy can move freely through our stillness, without overwhelming us. One student told me she no longer felt like a "walking whirlwind," manipulated and disoriented by powerful inner and outer currents. There are techniques for protecting ourselves from unwanted influences in the energy dimension, but these involve holding an image of a surrounding light or other protective boundary. These techniques diminish our direct experience of life because they involve a constant use of the imagination, and they also promote an attitude of fearfulness. They are not necessary when we live in the dimension of fundamental consciousness.

For example, a woman came to see me who had lived in a spiritual community for many years. She had recently stopped her meditation practice because she had had an experience that badly frightened her. She had felt such overpowering waves of love during her meditation that she was afraid she would go crazy if she allowed them to continue. When she learned how to attune to fundamental consciousness, she was able to let the waves of love pass through the unmoving space of her consciousness, without disturbing it. She experienced herself as steady and stable, and at the same time, she experienced the streaming energy of her open heart.

Once we are secure in our realization of fundamental consciousness, we can open without fear to our own energy and the energy around us. We are like an empty vessel. Whatever is in the vessel is temporary and does not alter our fundamental nature. No matter how powerful the movement of life becomes, it does not change the absolute stillness of fundamental consciousness.

This is the paradox of enlightenment. We receive the stimulation of our environment even more fully than before we were enlightened. Because we have more access to the depths of our self, we feel everything—joy and pain—more deeply than before. But at the same time, we experience our self as whole and steady, as the unchanging ground of fundamental consciousness. One of my teachers once likened this state to the Biblical burning bush. "We burn," he said, "but we are not consumed."

Our emotional pain is secondary to our fundamental nature. No matter what we lose or suffer in our life, this core of our being, our true reality, cannot be damaged. It has not moved from the beginning, and it will never move. Thus, as we become enlightened, it is easier to be at peace with even the worst of our circumstances. We can allow our self to mourn or rage, to risk new relationships and situations, because we know that our fundamental nature will always survive.

Summary

In summary, enlightenment is the realization of one's own nature as ultimate reality. It is a radical shift from the fragmentation of subject-object duality to the unity of our fundamental dimension of pure consciousness. This fundamental dimension is experienced as vast, clear, unbreakable, unbounded space, pervading both our body and our environment. Once we realize fundamental consciousness, our realization continues to deepen and expand throughout our lifetime. When we become enlightened, our own mind is continuous with the consciousness that is the basis of all existence, which has been its true nature all along. Our dimension of fundamental consciousness is always with us, at the root of our self and the universe, and we are all capable of realizing it.

2

Defining Self and Selflessness

RECENTLY I ATTENDED a discourse by a respected teacher of Eastern religion. He spoke forcefully about how our true nature is selfless and empty, or as he called it, void. The vibrant atmosphere in the room grew bleak as we contemplated our true non-existence and the nagging, persistent illusion of self in which this teacher knew we were all trapped. When it was over a man behind me stood and asked the teacher how a psychotherapist, like himself, could help his clients overcome this illusion. The teacher must have been used to this question because he answered immediately that psychotherapy misleads people from the start by regarding them as human beings. "If you tell someone they are a human being," he said, "you are already reinforcing their illusion of self."

Enlightenment is often described as a state of selflessness. This description is not, as we shall see, untrue in every way. But it has led to confusion on the part of many spiritual seekers, who obediently make up their minds to ignore their desires, judgments, emotions, personal quirks, and talents, to "block out" any sense of self; on hearing this teaching of selflessness, these seekers pretend that they don't exist. Ken Wilber, a leading psycho-spiritual theorist, writes that we cannot even enter the transpersonal realm until we "let go of personal life on the whole." Although Wilber himself may understand the nature of spiritual maturity, descriptions such as these have misled many people on the spiritual path. The difficulty arises out of a misinterpretation of the meaning of self and selflessness in the context of enlightenment.

The Eastern teaching of selflessness is often misunderstood to mean a state of non-existence, in which one ceases to experience oneself as a unique individual, or to experience oneself at all. The Dalai Lama has tried to bring clarity to the understanding of the self in Buddhism. In an interview with John F. Avedon, he says: "There are two types of 'I' or self: coarser and more subtle. There is the 'I' which is designated on the gross mind and body and that which is designated on the subtle mind and energy. When the one is active the other is not. . . . The coarse 'I' is designated in dependence on the coarse mind and body. But even when they are not operating, there has to be an 'I' designated. That is then designated to the subtle mind and body which are then present. For instance, a highly developed yogi who is able to manifest a subtler consciousness and at the same time view conventional phenomena, for that person there is an innate sense of 'I' —not in the coarser sense, but in a far more subtle sense—designated upon the subtle mind and body." John Avedon then asks the Dalai Lama, "What happens to the most subtle energy-mind when a being becomes enlightened?" The Dalai Lama replies, "The 'I' of a Buddha, the self of a Buddha, is this subtle 'I.'"

Selflessness is also often misunderstood, in the West, to mean unselfishness, or egolessness (in the sense of lack of conceit or concern for oneself). In the Western psyche the teaching of selflessness tends to evoke images of the self-denial and self-sacrifice of Christian saints.

Most of us were taught as children not to be selfish. When we hear what sounds like the same message from authority figures such as spiritual teachers, it touches our distant memory of these early admonitions, and may trigger unconscious fears of parental punishment. As I will address more fully in chapter 4, there is also a more subtle but just as common childhood injunction. This is the injunction against being fully oneself—a separate person with volition, feelings, desires, and cognitions of one's own. Although this teaching was most often unconscious on the part of our parents, the threatened punishment for transgression was usually too terrible to risk: loss of love and the sense of not belonging in one's own family (loss of recognition).

For example, one woman told me that she would be "so powerful" if she allowed herself to experience her own strength that she would surely overwhelm, and alienate, everyone who met her. In our continued conversations, she related the power struggles she had fought with her father, and the awful moment when she saw fear in his eyes, when she realized that he was now on the defensive instead of herself. She never allowed herself to feel any stronger than in that moment. And I remember another woman who wept when she experienced her intelligence, mourning the loss of her mother who had withdrawn from her, hurt and bewildered, when she began to develop her own mind. And the middle-aged man who had been the youngest of five children and still maintained the tight, unbreathing stance of someone trying "not to make any more waves," as he put it, in a chaotic household.

The process of individuation is fraught with psychological obstacles. As young children, the spontaneous self-love that springs from the enjoyment of our own senses and understanding often evokes pain or annoyance, even rage, in adults who have lost this self-love themselves. The sense of being separate, the privacy and psychological distance necessary to mature, is almost always intolerable to parents who themselves were not allowed psychological separation. Psychologists such as Alice Miller have found that children will sacrifice these basic components of selfhood to maintain the warmth and nourishment of their parents' love.

There are also social obstacles to our growing sense of self. Remember how only one little boy could tell that the emperor was naked? Our innate drive to think for ourselves and express our unique perspective on the world is hidden and forgotten for the sake of acceptance, for the comfort and safety of fitting in to our community. One man, as he began to experience the quality of his own being, asked, "Who will know me if I become myself?"

For many people, hearing or reading that they don't really exist, or should not exist if they want to be spiritual, causes them to further divorce themselves from their own experience and appreciation of themselves, to work harder at self-effacement and the diminishment of their personal qualities. They respond to the teaching of selflessness with the residual shame and guilt of their childhood. How can I get rid of my big, bad self? they want to know.

We are all familiar with the stereotype of feigned piety in Western religious traditions. Most often this sanctimonious, falsely smiling character does realize that he or she is pretending, but has simply been convinced that nothing less than perfect goodness is acceptable to the Lord. In similar fashion, when spiritual students are persuaded that enlightenment is non-existence, the result is too often a strangely vacant, emotionally flattened, unreal human being. The worst of this situation is that to limit our human reality is to limit our spiritual reality, for they are one and the same. Enlightenment is the true nature, the reality, of our humanness. We can only progress spiritually by becoming more real, not less.

There is certainly fear involved in releasing the psychological defenses that obscure our realization of fundamental consciousness, because they have given us a sense of safety since childhood, and we may *think* that we will cease to exist without them. But we do not cease to exist. As I will explain in this chapter, the process of releasing defenses and realizing fundamental consciousness increases our sense of self, our security in our self, and our sense of truly existing.

As we become enlightened, we have a profound sense of being real, for the first time. Our previous existence seems shadowy and illusory by comparison. In the dimension of fundamental consciousness, we know our self as the essential existence at the core of all life, we experience our self as life itself. There is nothing abstract or impersonal about this feeling of life. For it is our own skin that awakens to touch, our own chest that softens and fills with love. It is literally that we have been numb, in our sensations, our heart, and our awareness, and now we are waking from that numbness.

I have observed, working with people in the process of deepening enlightenment, that the greatest obstacle to spiritual maturity is not the fear of non-existence, but the fear of existing, of being fully alive, and of being one's own individual self. It should be said that spiritual practice also poses the danger that we will artificially inflate our sense of self, that we will pretend to be a superior being, with powers and knowledge beyond our true attainment. At root, however, this narcissistic attitude is also a fear of truly existing—of being real. Self-inflation is part of the false self that I will discuss below, compensating for a hollow, diminished sense of self. The sense of self that develops together with our realization of fundamental consciousness is an experience of becoming clear space, pervading evenly through our body and environment. It feels nothing like the static attitude of the narcissist which attempts to push against, or blot out, the outside world. Also, the experience of narcissism is largely conceptual—the narcissist convinces himself that he is superior. In his inflated posture he may feel that he is somehow higher up, or more expanded, than other people, but he will not experience the actual quality of self that is present in the realized self.

It is crucial for effective spiritual practice that we understand what is meant by the words "self" and "selflessness" in spiritual experience. To do this, we will now examine four different interpretations of these words that are often confused with each other: the true or essential self, the false self, ethical selflessness, and ultimate selflessness.

The Essential Self

The basic premise of this book is that there exists a true, or essential, sense of self which persists and grows with the realization of fundamental consciousness. In other words, as we attain a sense of ourselves as boundless, pervasive, pure consciousness, we have a simultaneous, precise awareness of our individual existence within this vast space. And as our boundlessness increases over time, so does our individuality. We become one with the environment and cos-mos, as we become separate. Although this sounds paradoxical, when we understand what actually occurs in the body and mind as we attain and deepen our enlightenment, it becomes easier to understand the co-existence of unbounded fundamental consciousness and individuality.

As I said in the first chapter, fundamental consciousness pervades all of our body as well as all of the environment. As we realize fundamental consciousness, we gain conscious access, or contact, with the inner space of our body. The more enlightened we become, the more inner space becomes available. We gradually become conscious throughout the inner volume, the inner content, of our whole body. Therefore, subject and object, or inner and outer life, although unified in the one pervasive field of fundamental consciousness, are clearly distinguishable from one another. Our fundamental consciousness, pervading and reflecting our inner and outer experience, is clearly conscious of where life inside of our individual form ends, and the life outside of our form begins.

I worked with a young artist who had a great resistance to experiencing fundamental consciousness pervading her. "I am already so open and vulnerable," she kept telling me. It was hard for her to believe that she would still feel intact as a separate person if she attuned to this core dimension of herself. Still, she persevered in the exercise (the first exercise described in chapter 1) of finding the space inside and outside her body, and feeling that they are the same, continuous space. Then one night she had a dream that illustrated her growing realization. She dreamt that she was seated on a beautiful upholstered chair in the middle of an oblong room. She noticed that the room had no walls; it was completely open. But seated in her chair, she felt secure. As we attune to fundamental consciousness in our body, we gain the security of self-knowledge and self-possession, the ability to "sit" in our self, even as we become unbounded.

In enlightenment, unity does not mean fusion. It does not mean that inner and outer space are somehow merged into one undifferentiated glob of experience. We do not confuse our own self with the window sill, or the trees, or the neighbors.

As fundamental consciousness, we pervade our own form, as well as the other forms in the environment. This produces a shift in the way we attune to the inner experience occurring in the life around us. Before we are enlightened, we have to rely on facial expressions, gestures, and words to know what other people are feeling. Or, as some very sensitive people report, we feel the feelings of others in our own body, where it is difficult to tell if they are our own feelings or someone else's. But when we are enlightened, our own consciousness is continuous with the fundamental consciousness of other people, animals, and plants. We can therefore focus within these forms to know the sensations, emotions, and eventually even the thoughts occurring there.

We have direct, in-depth contact with other life, and we feel great kinship with other life, because the core dimension of our own being is the same as the core of other life ("the whole universe is of one and the same root as my own self"). But our contact with other life occurs across space, from our own body to the body of another. If I feel someone else's grief, I know it is someone else's because it occurs somewhere else in the field of fundamental consciousness than in my own body. I may respond to that person's grief with grief in my own body, as often happens because we are empathic creatures, but I will be aware then of the sequence of another's grief and then my own. This may seem obvious to some readers, but many people misinterpret the boundlessness of enlightenment as meaning that there is no true distinction between one's own experience and another's.

Dramatic language is often used to describe enlightenment, such as "leaping off a cliff," or the "death" of the separate self. Like the comedian who joked that reports of his death had been exaggerated, I believe that reports of this "death" have also been greatly exaggerated, or at least misunderstood. To become unified with the whole of life does not eliminate our internal contact, or awareness of our separate subjectivity. Although all life is essentially one consciousness, we are obviously not all thinking the same thoughts. At least as long we are embodied and on Earth, as long as our attunement to fundamental consciousness is partial and incomplete, our existence is centered, and growing, within a separate, individual, self-referential form at the same time as it is unified with all other life.

The essential self that we gradually discover in the dimension of fundamental consciousness feels more substantial than the sense we have of our self before we are enlightened. The more our fundamental consciousness pervades the inner volume of our body, the more contact we gain with our individual form. There is simply more to us, more volume, more depth. We are coming to know our self in every cell.

But the substantiality of the essential self is not just a matter of volume. The essential self is made of pure consciousness, which is substantial in itself. The substantiality of essential being is described by contemporary theorist A.H. Almaas. He writes, "We have asserted the truth of substantiality to impress on the reader that essence or being is not a state of mind, but is an actual and palpable ontological presence."

The realization of our innate substantiality produces a very different and more comfortable way of being in the world. Many sensitive people tend to "flee the body" when outside stimuli seem too abrasive for them. This is a kind of scattering of consciousness, a rapid, reflexive disassociation from oneself. For example, my student Anna was very reactive to loud sounds. I was working with her in a quiet country setting, disturbed only by the occasional barking of dogs. She was working on inhabiting the space inside her body, when the dogs began a spirited dialogue with one another from their respective yards. Each time a dog barked, Anna would scatter her consciousness and disassociate from her body. She realized that she went through life continuously scattered in reaction to cars, neighbors, sirens, and other sounds in her environment. After careful practice, Anna was able to experience that the quality of her own being was more substantial than these sounds. She became secure and stable enough in her realization of fundamental consciousness to remain present and unchanged when sounds occurred. Fundamental consciousness cannot be harmed or in any way affected by inner or outer stimuli. It is always unbroken and unchanging. As Anna began to experience the substantiality of her essential self, all her inter- actions with the world were affected. She presented herself to others as someone with weight, with tangible value, because that is how she felt. And people responded to her with a new degree of attention and consideration.

The scattering of consciousness occurs severely during trauma such as sexual abuse. Recovery from sexual abuse is almost always a process of returning to inhabit the body after disassociating from it. I worked with a woman named Penelope who was sexually abused by her father throughout her childhood. She was now forty—attractive, friendly, and successful in her work. But she could not be physically touched. If a friend casually put a hand on her shoulder or touched her hand she would experience the same rapid scattering of consciousness that Anna felt in reaction to sounds. Penelope worked through intense emotions of terror, rage, shame, and revulsion as she regained conscious access to the inner space of her body. She spent weeks trying to tolerate being in her ankles, expressing the fury and urgency to kick that she felt when she was inside them. It was a full year before she could inhabit her sexual organs and feel safe. Penelope and I worked directly on her aversion to touch. She would practice remaining inside her wrist and hand, and experiencing the substantiality of her essential self in her wrist and hand, as I held my hand several inches above hers. Gradually she was able to maintain her realization of fundamental consciousness throughout her body, as I put my hand on her wrist. It is deeply healing for people who have been physically or sexually abused to realize that the innermost ground of their being has not been in any way harmed or altered by their attacker.

I have said that fundamental consciousness easily distinguishes our own inner life from the rest of the world it pervades, that it easily distinguishes our own form from the others. But the question remains: What enables fundamental consciousness to recognize our own particular life form as our own, and the other forms as not our own? If fundamental consciousness is truly unified, how do we know our own self from the tree, the chair, or the neighbor?

The contemporary Indian teacher Sathya Sai Baba has said that the "I" which we each experience is all the same "I" —it is all the one "I" that is pure consciousness. Fundamental consciousness has an inherent quality of "I"ness, a quality of "I exist." Yet we each experience this "I" as emanating from our own individual form, as the center of our own individual locus of being. As I have said, the more we mature in our realization of fundamental consciousness, the more clear and substantial this sense of self or "I" becomes. But it also becomes clearer that this self or "I" is emanating from the center of our own form. This is because we realize fundamental consciousness through the central core of our own body.

The subtle channel in the central, vertical core of the body is considered by both Buddhist and Hindu spiritual teaching to play an important role in spiritual development. It is called in Buddhism the *central channel* and in Hindu yoga *sushumna*, the central channel of the subtle nervous system (of which the chakras are also a part). The more access we gain to the vertical core of the body, the more space we gain in the dimension of fundamental consciousness. As I will ex-plain more fully in the next two chapters, enlightenment and individuation are both a process of penetrating inward to the center of our being. Thus individuation and enlightenment proceed in the same way, at the same time. They are really one and the same process.

Since we realize fundamental consciousness through the core of our body, the quality of "I" does emanate, just as we experience it, from the core of our individual being. We are each the center, and, in a sense, the origin or the wellspring, of the one "I" of fundamental consciousness. Although fundamental consciousness is truly unified, we each realize it at our own unique point in vast space. Our individual being, with its particular memories, talents, and defenses, is coiled around this point in space.

Most people live their whole lives without any contact with the vertical core of their own body. This is because our access to the core of our self is obstructed by psychological defenses—repressed memories and emotions that become embedded in the tissues of our body, making them too dense and rigid to be easily penetrated by our consciousness. One of my more humorous students told me, after his first experience of being in the vertical core of his body, "I've been most places in the world, but I've never been here before." All of us have easier access to some parts of the vertical core than to other parts of it, depending on our particular pattern of psychological defense. I will explain this more fully in the next chapter.

Everyone I have ever worked with has been able to recognize when they enter the vertical core of the body, for it has a very specific quality. It has a fine, electrical charge, and within that, a stillness and a quality of truth, or essence—a quality that one recognizes as one's true self that has always been there, but only dimly perceived, within all of one's experience. It feels like the very center of being, the center of all the pervasive space of fundamental consciousness.

EXERCISE 3   *Finding the Vertical Core of the Body*

Here is an exercise to help you contact and begin to live in the vertical core of your body.

> We enter the vertical core first in the center of the head. Mentally find the center of your head.
>
> This is an area between your ears and between your face and the back of your head, below the crown of your head. If your head were a perfect sphere, it would be right in the center of the sphere. Most of us in Western culture live a little above (and in front of) the center of the head. Make sure that you can feel the bottom of your torso *from* the center of your head. This will ensure that you are not above center. If you are in the center of your head, and not above it, the whole vertical core of your body will be contacted and stimulated by your being in the center of your head.
>
> Feel that the center of your head is in the center of the pervasive space of fundamental consciousness.
>
> Inhale through your nostrils and bring the breath into the center of your head. Then exhale through your nostrils.
>
> Make the breath smooth and very fine, (it should feel like it is half-breath, half-mind), and direct it precisely, like a laser beam, into the center of your head. If you have difficulty bringing breath into your head, begin by imagining the path of the breath. When this becomes very easy for you, integrate the breath with the image.
>
> Now initiate the breath from the center of your head. Let the

center of the head draw in the breath, something like sucking air through a straw. The exhale is a release of the breath from inside the center of your head.

Now find a point on the level of your heart but in the center of your chest, as interior in your body as you can focus. (This is the heart chakra in the Hindu yoga system.)

Feel that the heart center is in the center of the pervasive space of fundamental consciousness.

Keep your focus there and breathe smoothly in and out of your nose.

Now feel that the breath initiates in the heart center. The heart center draws in the breath. It feels as if the heart center is breathing in mind as well as breath, or as if the mind were breathing inside the heart center. The exhale is a release from inside the heart center.

Next, find the center of your pelvis, about two inches below your navel and as interior in your body as you can penetrate with your focus.

Feel that the pelvis center is in the center of the pervasive space of fundamental consciousness.

Hold your focus steady in this area and breathe smoothly through your nose.

Now feel that the breath initiates in the pelvis center. The pelvis center draws in the breath. Feel that the pelvis center breathes in mind and breath at the same time, or that the mind is breathing inside the pelvis center. Exhale by releasing the breath from inside the pelvis center.

Next, find all three centers (of your head, heart, and pelvis) at the same time. Be sure that you do not leave out the center of your head. Try to feel that the breath initiates in all three centers at the same time. All three centers draw in the breath. It feels as if the breath is mixed with mind, or that the mind is breathing inside the core of the body. Exhale by releasing the breath from inside all three centers at the same time.

Feel that the whole vertical core is in the center of pervasive space, inhaling and exhaling.

This exercise will help establish you in the essential self. The realization of the essential self requires a spatial shift in perspective from the periphery of the body to the vertical core.

Fundamental consciousness, as the ground of all our experience, contains all the essential qualities of our being. The vertical core of the body, as the entranceway to fundamental consciousness, is also the source of our essential qualities. Hindu yoga divides the vertical core's spectrum of qualities into seven main qualities associated with the seven main chakras. (The chakras are sensitive points along the vertical core where it is easiest to access the core.) Because the vertical core is a spectrum or continuum of qualities, it can be divided in any way. But any division is only schematic, for the purpose of understanding and cultivating the entire spectrum.

In Subtle Self Work I divide the vertical core into three qualities: awareness, emotion (or love), and physical sensation. Physical sensation is attuned to through the bottom third of the vertical core, emotion through the middle third of the core, and awareness through the upper third of the core.

These three qualities do not refer to specific awarenesses, emotions, or sensations, but to the underlying ground of fundamental consciousness within which specific experiences occur. In other words, fundamental consciousness, containing the qualities of awareness, emotion, and sensation, pervades and reflects specific awarenesses, emotions, and sensations. Specific experiences are transitory and contingent upon causes, but the underlying fundamental consciousness is stable and enduring.

Each of the qualities of awareness, emotion, and sensation pervade the entire body and the entire field of fundamental consciousness (the entire universe). This is difficult to visualize or to grasp conceptually, but it is not difficult to experience. Each of the three qualities can be focused on separately, as you will see in the following exercise, but they are actually inseparable. Every moment of our experience contains awareness, emotion, and physical sensation, even if we are not conscious of all these qualities. The field of fundamental awareness, emotion, and sensation pervades our entire body (even if we have not realized it) and it also pervades everything in nature. This means that every rock, tree, animal, or star is pervaded by awareness, emotion, and sensation, even if they do not realize it.

Depending upon our particular design of psychological defense and conditioning, we are each more open and more habituated to living in some of these qualities than others. The following exercise will help you understand how you have been accustomed to experiencing life, and help you realize the qualities that have been less accessible for you. For the total realization of fundamental consciousness, all of these qualities must be realized. Therefore, no part of the vertical core is more important for spiritual maturity (or the process of individuation) than any other part.

EXERCISE 4 *Qualities of Fundamental Consciousness*

Begin by repeating exercise 1 from the first chapter: Feel that you are inside your whole body all at once. Mentally find the space outside your body. Experience that the space inside and outside your body is the same, continuous space; it pervades you.

Now I am going to ask you to attune to three different qualities of fundamental consciousness: awareness, emotion, and physical sensation. You will get best results from this exercise if you do not question intellectually what I mean by these qualities. Simply *intend* to experience them and then observe yourself closely for changes in the quality of your experience.

For most people, this subtle level of attunement and self-observation is new. By repeated intentions to refine our experience, the new "wiring" becomes available.

Attune to the quality of awareness. This means to become aware of being aware. Awareness is the ground of all our mental activity. Another name for this quality is clarity. You will find that you attune to the quality of awareness through the upper third of the vertical core of your body.

Experience that the quality of awareness pervades your whole body and the whole environment.

This is the ground of awareness, within which specific, transient thoughts, intuitions, and images occur.

Attune to the quality of emotion. This will be a different experience than the quality of awareness. The difference might be described as a change in texture, or weight. The quality of emotion is attuned to through the middle third of the vertical core. In its most refined state (that is, when we are most open to it), the quality of emotion is experienced as pure love, or bliss. But do not try to feel bliss; let your quality of emotion feel just as it does. For most of us, our attunement to bliss is diminished by the emotions held in our psychological defenses. You may feel some of these repressed emotions as you attune to the fundamental quality of emotion, but the fundamental quality is itself unchanged by our specific emotions. With practice you can experience your specific emotions as secondary patterns in the pervasive ground of fundamental consciousness.

Now experience that the quality of emotion pervades your whole body and the whole environment. (Love is everywhere, even in the air.)

This is the ground of emotion, within which specific, transient emotions move.

Attune to the quality of physical sensation. This again is a different experience than emotion or awareness. You will find that your focus moves down to the bottom third of your vertical core as you attune to physical sensation. The fundamental quality of physical sensation is the ground of all our specific physical sensations. If you have difficulty experiencing it, try looking at an object near you and seeing its texture. Living in the quality of physical sensation brings texture to our experience of the world. The quality of physical sensation is often not addressed in spiritual disciplines, but it is an essential aspect of our individual wholeness, our communion with other people, and our oneness with nature.

Now experience the quality of physical sensation pervading your whole body (including your head), and pervading the whole environment.

Attune to the qualities of awareness and physical sensation at the same time, pervading your whole body and environment. Now add in the quality of emotion, so that all three qualities are pervading your whole body and environment.

Sit for a moment in this rich field of fundamental awareness, emotion, and sensation, allowing your breath to glide through the space without disturbing or altering your attunement to it. As fundamental consciousness, you are unified with the fundamental awareness, love, and sensation of everything in the universe.

You may remember that in exercise 1, the exercise called for you to attune to the qualities of gender, power, love, voice, and understanding. When the awareness, emotion (or love), and sensation of fundamental consciousness pervades the body, it becomes further delineated into those qualities. For example, although fundamental consciousness itself cannot be said to contain gender, our embodied essential self does have a particular male or female quality. Some of the most prevalent wounding in human beings is to this essential sense of gender. Among other reasons, the exaggerated cultural stereotypes of both maleness and femaleness cause many people to cut themselves off from this quality of their being. But by attuning to fundamental consciousness in our lower torso, we can regain this essential aspect of ourselves. This is important in part because if we constrict our sense of gender, we also limit our capacity for sexual pleasure.

People often live more in one or two qualities of fundamental consciousness, while "blocking off" and defending the third. I worked with a young dancer named Bella who was only comfortable when she was moving. During our sessions, she would slide off the couch and hang over, stretching and flexing her muscles. She was unable to sit and look at me while we talked. She was also unable to have the intimate friendships and love that she craved.

We discovered that Bella had been a particularly sensitive child, acutely aware of the emotions and needs of the people around her. She described her mother as loving but frantic, with a "high frequency" showing in her eyes that disturbed Bella greatly. Her mother also depended on Bella as her primary source of love, a role that Bella felt inadequate to fill.

When Bella attuned to the three qualities of fundamental consciousness, she was able to experience physical sensation very easily. Emotion was a little more difficult, but the quality of awareness felt threatening even to attempt. She realized that she kept herself in almost constant motion so that she would not experience awareness. When I moved to the other side of the room and averted my gaze, Bella finally felt safe enough to attune to the quality of awareness. She then recognized that her fear of awareness was a fear of becoming aware of other people's pain, and feeling responsible for alleviating their pain.

Another client named Paul had the most difficulty attuning to physical sensation, while the quality of awareness was the easiest for him. He was a large man with muscular shoulders, but his demeanor was timid and extremely polite, as if he were trying not to offend me.

Paul had grown up with a violent father who abused his wife, bragged about his affairs with other women, and dominated the family. When Paul attuned to physical sensation he said he felt like his father and he was afraid that he would be capable of the same destructive power. Over time, Paul was able to feel his own sensuality and power, without his father's attitude of sexual aggression and rage.

When people experience their fundamental qualities for the first time, they begin to feel both trust and appreciation towards themselves. This deep contact with oneself is the basis of true self-esteem and, as such, it brings significant healing to all psychological maladies. When we truly know ourselves, we are able to trust ourselves with intimacy, material success, artistic expression, and the various responsibilities of mature life. Also, when we can feel that an essential aspect of our own being is love, our yearning for the love we did not receive from important people in our childhood becomes more tolerable.

Although many psychologists have referred to a true or essential self, A.H. Almaas is one of the few theorists to describe it as an experienced reality. But if I am understanding him correctly, he makes a distinction between the "personal essence" and transcendent consciousness. This view I believe is inaccurate, and represents a prevalent error in this field of study. Almaas refers to transcendent consciousness as "Impersonal Being" or the "Impersonal Witness," describing it like this: "One experiences oneself as an emptiness that has no characteristic except that of being a totally silent Impersonal Witness. There is a stupendous vastness, an absolute silence, a complete impersonality, and a singularly clear but absolutely uninvolved awareness of everything."

I do not believe that transcendent consciousness is in any way different or separate from the essential self. Hindu philosophy uses the word Atman for the essential self. The Hindu scholar Chandradhar Sharma writes, "We have seen that the same reality is called from the subjective side as Atman and from the objective side as Brahman. The two terms are synonymous. The Absolute of the Upanishads manifests itself as the subject as well as the object and transcends them both."

The difficulty that all writers on this subject have is that we are attempting to describe that which is essentially experiential. Almaas's description of the Impersonal Witness sounds like an experience of attunement to fundamental consciousness through only the upper portion of the vertical core of the body. In other words, it is attunement to the quality of awareness without the qualities of emotion and physical sensation.

It is important to understand that the dimension of fundamental consciousness contains the very essence of our humanness—aware-ness, emotion, and physical sensation. To realize fundamental consciousness is an exquisitely personal experience, at the same time that it unifies and transcends the subject-object dichotomy. Although it may sound paradoxical until you have experienced it, fundamental consciousness is simultaneously an experience of personal separate-ness and transcendent oneness with the foundation of all life.

To be an essential self means that with each breath we breathe our fundamental awareness, emotion, and physical sensation. This is the self that is beyond ideas, that is not abstract but actual. In sum-mary, the essential self is an experience of personal individuality because:

1. It is discovered by penetrating inward to our own individual core.
2. It pervades and reflects our individual body.
3. It contains the essential qualities associated with our humanness.
4. It is the underlying, pervasive sense of "I" that we each recognize as our own true self, and which becomes clearer and more substantial as we progress in our realization.

Once we have begun to be enlightened, we each realize fundamental consciousness with different parts of our vertical core, depending on our individual design of defense and openness. We each experience the one, unified dimension of fundamental consciousness from our own unique perspective. It is these varying perspectives that make reality a "relative" reality. Reality itself does not change; it is always ultimate reality. In fact, the terms ultimate and reality are synonymous. But our experience of reality is relative and partial. Since our essential self is fundamental consciousness, our experience of our essential self is also relative and partial. As we progress in our realization, however, we move in the direction of attuning to fundamental consciousness through the entire core of our body, and of knowing our essential self completely. We move towards ultimate reality.

The False Self

The false self is an amalgam of images, concepts, defensive attitudes, and bound childhood pain which we mistake for our identity. Rather than having the felt sense of our existence described in the last section, we have an imagined idea of who we are. We live in a "dream" in which our true center of reference is deserted and hollow.

The behaviors and attitudes of the false self were created to cope with painful or confusing aspects of the external world. They were designed to attract love and avoid pain in specific, repeated situations in our past. As children, we distort our true responses and needs in order to become the child that our parents will recognize and appreciate, and to protect ourselves from feeling abandoned, misunderstood, shamed, deprived, and so on. Daniel Stern in *The Interpersonal World of the Infant* describes the forming of the false self as the "center of gravity shifting from inside to outside." As we will examine more closely in the next chapter, the false self does not develop in isolation. It is a distortion of the self in interaction with the environment—an entanglement of self and other.

The false self is made of many levels of distortion. Painful emotion and memory are kept from consciousness by a process of binding and constriction in the mental, energetic, and physical dimensions of our organism. This binding preserves the emotion and memory in our body, where it continues to color or "haunt" our subsequent perceptions and responses. The binding of our mental, energetic, and physical instrument also creates gaps in our ability to experience life, which are compensated for with false images of our self and our environment.

These false images engender a system of false beliefs that, although unconscious or barely conscious, influence all of our life choices. For example, someone who is repeatedly criticized as a child may close the tissue of his body around a feeling of shame. He may then hold an image of himself as a worthless person, or a compensatory image of himself as a superior person. He may form a rigid belief that if people get to know him they will also be critical of him, and may avoid close relationships with people. Or someone who felt abandoned as a child may close her heart around her grief and cover this feeling with a static pretense of apathy, or a sentimentalized love for others which is not, and cannot be, actually felt in her heart. She may also carry a dimly conscious belief that life is inherently sad, and that one can never be truly loved. The human imagination provides many variations on the themes of defense, compensation, and belief.

The static distortions of the false self become, over time, static patterns of tension in the body which literally trap us in their limiting patterns. In Subtle Self Work I call these static patterns of tension *densities* because they are actual densities in the fascia, or connective tissue, of our body. These densities obscure our realization of fundamental consciousness. They block our access to the vertical core of the body, and they impede our spontaneous, direct experience of life. They keep us reacting to the world as we reacted, out of what was then necessity, in our family of origin.

The various static attitudes and complexes of behavior that make up the false self have led some theorists to conclude that a person is made up of many different personalities. But it is really only the false self that is made of different personalities. The essential self that one discovers in enlightenment is whole and unified.

The word "ego" is often used to denote the false self. The teaching of selflessness is then spoken of as an attempt to be egoless, and enlightenment is seen as the death of the ego. But the word ego is used in so many different ways that this teaching is also a source of confusion. For example, the word ego is sometimes used to mean self-love or conceit. But self-love can be either false and compensatory (for lack of self-love), or it can be the healthy, spontaneous response to a felt sense of one's essential self.

The word "ego" is also used to mean the ability to organize one's environment, to navigate and discriminate, to make choices, to persevere towards specific goals, and so forth. Traditional psychologists point to these abilities as signs of what they call "ego strength." Many spiritual students are led to believe that the abilities associated with ego strength are in the way of their progress and need to be eliminated.

This confusion is further compounded by the fact that traditional psychology also views ego strength as the ability to defend oneself psychologically, and to create "psychic structures" by internalizing images of the external world. This topic will be taken up more fully in the next chapter. Here I will only say that clear distinction must be made between the defensive activity of the wounded false self/ego and the self-confidence and volitional and cognitive abilities of the essential self, which continue to develop with spiritual growth. There is a vast difference between the skillful navigation of the essential self and the frightened manipulation of the false self.

It is the false self that gradually dissolves as we realize fundamental consciousness. As the densities of the false self are released, our body becomes increasingly permeable. What had seemed like our self now feels like it is dissolving in space. The barrier between the inside of our body and the outer world is replaced by a perception of unity, a simultaneous perception of inner and outer experience.

If a rapid shift occurs from a defended stance to the permeability of the essential self, it can feel like a loss of self, and may be frightening. However, it is most often a gradual change. The maturing individual has a chance to mourn the loss of old attachments and projections, and to appreciate the new directness of experience and the new type of substantiality that comes with the essential self.

As I have said, the realization of fundamental consciousness and the essential self is gradual and relative. This means that virtually everyone has some psychological entanglement and defense against life. A.H. Almaas writes, "The old idea is that the personality is the barrier and must be removed before there can be recognition of essential beingness. Our findings indicate that essence can be realized in steps, or in degrees, simultaneously with work on the personality."

It is crucial to our spiritual progress that we become aware of the remnant of childhood mentality in our behavior. If we know our own history of childhood pain, and how we tend to project it onto present situations, then we can gain flexibility in our behavior. Gradually we can release our childhood pain from its binding in our body, and see through the images and beliefs that this pain has engendered. But the first step is to become aware that it is there, so that we are not fooled by our own projections. For example, we may expect everyone in a position of authority to be dominating and potentially humiliating. If we do not become aware of the basis of this expectation, such as our early experience with a dominating, humiliating parent or teacher, we will approach all authority with an attitude of fear or anger. This attitude obscures our direct experience of the present-day situation. If we know about the relationship of our false self to authority, we may still feel fear or anger but we will know that this is not necessarily the appropriate response, and we can choose not to act on it.

The false self is based primarily on the repressed or denied needs and emotions of our childhood. Therefore it is not helpful for our growth to further deny these needs and emotions in an effort to be "selfless." The false self is bound up in our mind, energy and body. It does not go away when it is denied. Our innate drive for wholeness causes this bound part of our self to constantly seek expression in our behavior, dreams, illnesses, and, as I will explain in the final chapter of this book, even our circumstances. Only our consciousness, our acknowledgment, of these bound parts of our self can free us from their spell.

Effective psychotherapy allows us to give expression to the emotions and needs of the false self, and to release the defensive binding of our mind, energy, and body. As we are able to witness these fragmented, childhood parts of our self, our perspective deepens and allows us to finally access the vertical core of our body and the dimension of fundamental consciousness.

The fact that psychologists are increasingly speaking of psychological problems in terms of true self and false self has opened the way to recognizing and making use of the interface of psychological and spiritual disciplines. However, most psychologists, such as Alice Miller, Heinz Kohut, and D.W. Winnicott, seem much more articulate on the nature of the false self than the true self. To understand and experience the essential self requires knowledge of the fundamental dimension of consciousness. For the essential self is not just a type of functioning. It is an ontological presence capable of experiencing itself.

Ethical Selflessness

The Eastern spiritual teaching of selflessness is often misinterpreted as unselfishness. In general, Western religious teachings have emphasized ethical behavior rather than self-realization (enlightenment). The spiritually mature person is pictured as someone who always puts the needs of others before their own, who has no thought or concern for their own welfare. Our most respected spiritual figures have been people who exemplified ethical ideals, such as Mother Teresa, rather than people who presented themselves as realized beings.

The practice of selfless service to others is an important component of Eastern religion as well. In Mahayana Buddhism, for example, the practitioner vows not to reach total enlightenment until all sentient beings have also reached it. This is the ultimate sacrifice, stretching over many lifetimes, but manifesting in the present as the commitment to living so that one always furthers (and never hinders) the enlightenment of others.

Ethical selflessness is a path towards enlightenment, but it is not enlightenment itself. Mother Teresa herself has said that she is engaged in service for the sake of her soul. Selfless service refers to a mode of behavior. Even the state of goodness, or the general attitude of benevolence, describes a person's intention to perform good and benevolent acts. It does not describe a person's experience of being. But enlightenment (essential selfhood) is an experience of being.

The point I want to emphasize is that the experience of our essential self does not diminish our capacity for selfless service. It does not make us selfish to experience that we truly exist, and to develop in the direction of truly existing. In fact, the experience of our essential self is conducive to, if not necessary for, unselfish behavior. This is because the essential self is relatively disentangled (psychologically) from the environment. The person who lives in fundamental consciousness makes fewer projections of childhood pain onto present circumstances. She or he is less likely to be motivated by unmet childhood needs for love and approval, and therefore has more freedom to be truly generous. Also, as we experience our unity with other life, in the dimension of fundamental consciousness, we feel an inherent kinship with everything in nature. We are thus more likely to feel genuine concern for the people, animals, and vegetation in our environment. As our perspective deepens, we are more able to see the pain in the life around us, and we can also sometimes see the reasons for this pain. We then become better equipped to solve the problems in our society. There is also a more subtle and more spontaneous level of ethical behavior experienced in the dimension of fundamental consciousness, but I will leave that subject for chapter 6.

Ultimate Selflessness

The last type of selflessness we will look at is ultimate selflessness. In my understanding, when a traditional Eastern teaching refers to the metaphysical concept of selflessness, it is either referring to a lack of false self, or to this ultimate state. As for the nature of ultimate selflessness, we can only speculate, based on the observable direction of spiritual development. Eastern teachings suggest that from the perspective of ultimate reality, there is no individual self. That is, when we reach total enlightenment, which all the teachings agree is extremely rare, our separate, individual subjectivity entirely ceases to exist. Based on my own observations of the enlightenment process, I believe that total enlightenment depends upon the complete release of all psychological defenses, and the complete embodiment of our individual form.

The Eastern teaching of reincarnation says that our individual personality persists from lifetime to lifetime as a subtle body, imprinted with our major memories, personal tendencies, desires, and attachments. These imprints produce life circumstances for their fulfillment or resolution. They are the densities in our consciousness that obscure our realization of fundamental consciousness. In other words, our individual form exists because it is not yet fully realized, not yet fully pervaded with fundamental consciousness. According to the Eastern metaphysics, once we have resolved our conflicts, desires, and attachments, we have attained complete enlightenment and we are no longer reborn.

For example, the classic Hindu Vedantic text, *Ashtavakra Samhita*, says, "Know that which has form to be unreal and the formless to be permanent. Through this spiritual instruction you will escape the possibility of rebirth."

This quote, like other traditional Hindu teachings, equates permanence with reality and impermanence with unreality. All forms in nature are constructed from causes, such as seeds, sun, water, and so on, and are thus subject to destruction. All forms in nature are made of components, such as cells, atoms, and particles, and are thus subject to dissolution and decay. Therefore, when the Eastern teachings say the individual self is unreal, they mean that it is impermanent and will come to an end.

But it is not until we have completely accessed the vertical core of our body and completely pervaded our individual form as our essential self, that we dissolve the outline of our individuality—that we lose our location, our locus of perspective in the unified field of fundamental consciousness. Until then, there is always an inward center of reference, a deepening sense of self; in Daniel Stern's words, there is a "unifying subjective perspective," that answers to the pronoun "I." This self is translucent, permeable, and made of the clear, rich space of fundamental consciousness. It reflects the depths and boundaries of our individual form and at the same time, it pervades and reflects the whole of our environment.

It is important that we do not attempt to pretend to have come to an ultimate realization of selflessness, for this is not possible without the full realization of our individual form. The beginning of enlightenment is available to anyone who wants it. But total enlightenment is a goal so far in the distance that it is really only a direction, a state of omniscience, omnipotence, and omnipresence that we only very gradually approach.

Conclusion

Fundamental consciousness is the ground of existence, with the essential qualities of awareness, emotion, and sensation. It is the basis of our essential sense of self, the "I"ness at the core of our being. It is the Self, capital S, but it is experienced in each of us as the self, our own self. We all have an innate yearning for expression of the self, for contact with the self, for fruition of the self.

As we realize fundamental consciousness, we gain more sense of truly existing, even though the superficial signposts of our identity lose credibility for us. We may fear that we will lose our self if we give up our superficial, defensive identity, but it is not so. We actually feel more substantial and more present than in our defensive state. Before we realize our essential self, we often have difficulty knowing our own feelings and desires, and we can be easily manipulated and confused by the world around us. But when we experience our essential self, we have direct access to even our most subtle responses and needs, which we easily distinguish from the demands of the environment.

Fundamental consciousness pervades our being like a mirror, or witness, to everything that occurs in us, and allows us to know our self intimately and specifically. Therefore, becoming enlightened does not at all mean to lose the specific qualities of our individual self.

Enlightenment is sometimes called selflessness because there is no image or concept of the self in it, but only the self itself. The essential self, as I have described in this chapter, is not vacant but vividly alive and personal.

To be unified with the environment does not mean to merge our own identity with the environment. As long as we are embodied and on Earth, we each have some imbalance, some incompleteness that has not yet spun out into fundamental consciousness. It is as if we are each coiled around our own point in fundamental consciousness. We are like the warps in the fabric of space that Einstein wrote about.

Our point in space, our individual design of defense and openness, gives us each a unique perspective on life, a unique way of experiencing life, and our own path towards complete enlightenment.

EXERCISE 5   *Experiencing the Quality of Self*

Here is an exercise to help you experience the quality of self. If you do not think about what this means, but try to attune to the quality, you will probably find that you can actually experience a particular quality that feels like your self. This quality has always been with us, in the depths our life's activities and perceptions. It is the quality of fundamental consciousness which pervades all of our experience.

This exercise is almost the same sequence as exercise 1 from the previous chapter. Sit upright on a chair or pillow.

Begin by breathing smoothly and evenly through your nostrils.

Bring your attention down to your feet and feel that you are inside your feet, that you inhabit your feet. Now attune to the quality of your self inside your feet.

Feel that you are inside your ankles. Attune to the quality of your self inside your ankles.

Feel that you are inside your knees. Attune to the quality of your self inside your knees.

Feel that you are inside your thighs. Attune to the quality of your self inside your thighs.

Feel that you are inside your pelvis. Attune to the quality of your self inside your pelvis.

Feel that you are inside your midsection, between your ribs and your pelvis. Attune to the quality of your self inside your midsection.

Feel that you are inside your chest. Attune to the quality of your self inside your chest.

Feel that your are inside your shoulders, arms, and hands.

Attune to the quality of your self inside your shoulders, arms, and hands.

Feel that you are inside your neck. Attune to the quality of your self inside your neck.

Feel that you are inside your head—inside your face and your brain. Attune to the quality of your self inside your head.

Feel that you are inside your whole body all at once.

Attune to the quality of the pronoun "I" as deeply as you can in your body.

As that "I," let yourself let go of everything else. This "I" in the depths of your body is aware of your inner experience and the outer world, but it has no entanglement, no grasp on your inner or outer experience.

Mentally find the space outside of your body.

Experience that the space outside and inside your body is the same, continuous space.

Many people ask me why I use the words "self" or "I" in this exercise, rather than words like "essence" or "Buddha-nature." Essence, Buddha-nature, cosmic consciousness, emptiness, and many other terms have been used in spiritual literature to describe the experience of fundamental consciousness. I use the words self and I because the other words are concepts; they do not evoke an experience, except perhaps of blankness. But fundamental consciousness is not an experience of blankness. It feels like our self.

3

The Healing Process:
Freeing the Causal Body

Do away with your superimposition carefully and with
patience.

— Shankara

IN THE PREVIOUS two chapters I have said that there is a unified,
fundamental consciousness pervading the universe and all its
forms, and that this fundamental consciousness in our own body is
the basis of the essential self. In this chapter, we will look at the
relation of psychological healing to the realization of fundamental
consciousness.

There are two interdependent components of personal growth
which can be called the healing process and the realization process.
The healing component of personal growth involves the resolution
and release of painful memories and emotions held in the body,
along with the beliefs, projections, and defenses that result from
these held memories. The realization component of personal growth
is the natural progression from the infant's budding sense of essential self and other to the spiritual maturity of the fully realized
essential self and transcendent oneness with the universe.

Although we can only guess at the nature of the infant's experience, it seems obvious that, compared to adults, he is undefended, open to life, and must have some direct sense of himself and the environment. And it is equally obvious that his experience is only the barest shadow of the realization of a spiritually mature adult. A.H. Almaas writes, "A baby does experience essence, but for the adult it will be more developed, more expanded, more distinct, more powerful, and it will function in ways that are only a potential in a baby."

The gradual expanding of the realization of the essential self and transcendent unity with the environment is as natural and spontaneous a process as a flower seed unfolding its completed form. Both Zen Buddhism and the Dzog-chen school of Tibetan Buddhism make it clear that one only needs to sit still and breathe in order to become enlightened. In the last chapter I will speak more about how the forces in the universe pull our organism towards the perfect balance that is the completion of our individual form.

The inevitable painful events of infancy and childhood that become bound in the tissues of our body thwart the natural deepening of our breath and consciousness towards the vertical core of our body, and the realization of fundamental consciousness. As virtually no human being gets through childhood without some binding of pain in the body, the two processes of healing and realization occur simultaneously. As we release our psychological pain the natural movement towards enlightenment is able to occur.

How Emotional Pain Becomes Bound in the Body

People often ask why it is necessary to uncover their childhood pain, why it is not sufficient to change their current beliefs and behaviors in order to be happy. The binding of painful memory and emotion in the body is a binding of our instrument of experience, a contraction of our potential for awareness, emotion, and physical sensation. As long as our body, energy, and consciousness are bound up in the past, they are not available for present experience. We are unable to inhabit our body, to know our self fully, to fully pervade our body as our essential self, as long as these contractions or densities of memory, emotion, and physical body exist in our being. It is usually necessary to know our childhood history in order to precisely contact and release our bound pain.

For example, a woman told me that when she was trying to learn new skills or express herself publicly, she often felt as if a demon were attacking her. She had a vague sense in her body of cringing away from this shadowy figure. But it was not until she saw this demon clearly that she recognized the jealous rage in her mother's eyes and remembered the sickening, terrifying smell of whisky on her breath. She was then able to let her body move fully into the cringe, and to experience the childhood mentality that held her body in this extreme defensive posture. In other words, she experienced the consciousness, emotion, and physical movement of that terrifying memory, while witnessing this younger part of herself with her present-day consciousness. When she did this, she was able, from her childhood mentality, to release her body out of the cringe, and to feel, to finally discharge, the bound terror from her body.

Usually the process of releasing a bound childhood memory occurs over time and involves repeated experiences of the contraction in the body, as well as a resolution of the childhood material. The woman just described had to come to terms with her mother's alcoholic fury, the nurturing she had missed, and the decisions she had made about her own incompetence, based on her mother's attacks. Just knowing the true identity of her demon, and recognizing that it belonged to her past, made her less susceptible to its influence. She was able to begin to express and develop herself even before her cringing attitude and the memory of the attacks on her were entirely released.

However, it is important to understand that insight and changed behavior are not enough for actual personal growth. We do not gain access to the vertical core of our body; we do not proceed towards or deepen our realization of fundamental consciousness, unless our bound consciousness, emotion, and body are released. When we reconnect with a bound fragment of our self, the childhood mentality in the fragment is reunited with and expands our present-day consciousness. The released emotion frees and increases our energy system, and the released physical tension increases our physical comfort and health. We gain more of our unconditioned, essential being: more availability for awareness, emotional depth, and sensation. We even look different. As I will describe in chapter 5, our body appears smoother and more unified as we release our psychological pain.

To the sensitive eye, we all look, to some extent, like Picasso's cubist portraits. The permeable field that is our consciousness, energy, and body contain hardened, static patterns (the false self) in a complex composite of postures, expressions, and ages. For example, one pattern may be a grief-stricken young child; another a stunned, over-stimulated infant; a third, a furious school-age child, and so on. In a normal conversation with an adult, these various fragments may all communicate their separate messages at once, in the rapid flickering of facial expression, vocal tone, emotional vibration and physical attitude. The infant may communicate, "Please don't give me any more information, I can't take it," while the school-age child shuts me out with a defiant glare and the grieving young child begs for love.

Some of the patterns in our field of being are simply lines of movement, well-traveled paths of response to painful circumstances that happened repeatedly in childhood and that are "triggered" by similar situations in the present. If these patterns are repeated often enough they begin to rigidify in the physical body. The fascia (connective tissue) that pervades the body as the interface between energy and body hardens along the lines of the repeated pattern. These patterns, as I have said, preserve the memory, the mentality of our age, and the emotion of our bound response to the painful circumstances. Our patterns of response also rigidify in our body if they occur when we are very young (the younger we are, the more impressionable) or if our emotional response to a situation is extremely painful (if the trauma is severe).

The bound patterns in our body contain not only the painful moments of our childhood, but also defensive or compensatory attitudes that have been formed to protect us from further injury, such as the hypervigilant attitude of someone who was often abused, or the superior attitude of the narcissistic person who is compensating for the feelings of hurt and shame that he also holds in his body. Recently I worked with a woman who always kept a bright, uplifted expression on her face, no matter what she was saying. When I looked closely, I saw an edge of defiant bravery in this expression, and the sense of a young teenager. At the same time, there was a painful sadness in her chest and eyes, and the sense of a lonely, despairing child. Although she was able to feel these held postures easily when they were pointed out to her, she had for years looked out at the world with these two static expressions, unaware of either of them. As she began to experience them more fully, she remembered feeling "darker and more complex" than her teenage peers, and making an effort to appear more upbeat in order to fit in with them.

It is not always necessary to uncover the exact circumstances that produced a static attitude, as long as the attitude can be precisely contacted and experienced. An interesting example of this was the young man who came to work with me because he seemed unable to make money. He told me that his most important goal was to become financially secure but he always sabotaged the advancement of his career. We worked for several months to uncover his negative associations with material wealth, but made little progress. Although he wanted very much to resolve this problem, he often seemed determined not to change. Then one day in our session I saw seated in front of me a character who was as serene and simple, with downward gaze and deflated chest, as the most devoted Christian monk. Here was the fragment of this man that carefully avoided the temptation of material success. We never found out how he formed this attitude. Neither he nor his parents had been religious Christians. It is possible that he mirrored the attitude of his grandmother, a devout Catholic, whom he knew when he was very young. He is convinced that he formed his monk posture in past lifetimes. Whatever the truth of its origins, once he was able to consciously experience it, he was able to release it. In the process, he became interested in Christianity for a time, and finally rejected the pious ideal of poverty as inappropriate for the circumstances of his present life. At the same time, a subtle transformation occurred in his body. His upper chest expanded and filled with energy, dissolving the slight downward quality that had made him seem somewhat passive and withdrawn.

Our bound fragments of mentality, emotion, and body maintain their existence because they are cut off from our consciousness. They live in the past, until our present-day consciousness is literally reunited with them. It is not enough to know about our bound fragments. *They must be experienced in order to be released.* When our consciousness connects with the mentality of the fragment, it is no longer fragmented. When we can feel the old emotion in the fragment, we can finally discharge it. When our body returns to the contracted posture, we can access the old command to contract those muscles and relax them.

The Metaphysics of Emotional Binding

The understanding that emotional pain is bound in the body has existed in the field of psychotherapy since its beginning. Sigmund Freud described several cases of psychological trauma resulting in physical symptoms. His student, Wilhelm Reich, made the phenomenon of body-mind connection the focus of his life's work. He became the first psychotherapist to write about a relationship between traumatic childhood memories (and the energy of their emotional content) and rigidities in the physical body. He called the rigidities "character armor," saying that "character armor and muscular armor are functionally identical." He said that the character armor was arranged in segments, in horizontal rings around the body.

Reich discovered a sensation of streaming in the body which he called *orgone* or vegetative energy. He felt that this energy was the fundamental stratum of life. (The physics of his day was also discovering the energetic stratum of the universe.) He described character armor as "the result of a binding of vegetative energy." "In armored human organisms," he wrote, "the orgone energy is bound in the chronic contraction of the muscles."

Reich claimed that there could be no psychological healing unless the emotional charge of the memories was liberated from the muscular armoring. He wrote, "I have also explained why remembering traumatic experiences is not essential for orgone therapy. It serves little purpose unless accompanied by the corresponding emotion. The emotion expressed in the movement [of release] is more than sufficient to make the patient's misfortunes comprehensible, quite apart from the fact that the remembrances emerge of themselves when the therapist works correctly." Reich then goes on to raise a fascinating question. He writes, "What remains puzzling is how unconscious memory functions can be dependent upon the conditions of plasmatic [cellular] excitation, how memories can be preserved, so to speak, in plasmatic awareness."

Today, almost fifty years later, many schools of bodywork and psychotherapy have incorporated Reich's idea that painful memories are preserved in the body. Bioenergetics, Core energetics, Ida Rolf's Structural Integration, A.H. Almaas's theory of "holes" in the body, Rebirthing, and Holotropic Breathwork, among others, have all reported a correlation between bodily tension and repressed memories, and the healing effect of releasing the emotional charge of the memories from the body.

But today it still remains a mystery how painful memory is preserved in the body, and what exactly connects memory, energy, and the physical body. Although we need more research into this subject, I believe we can approach an understanding if we include in our formulation the underlying, pervasive dimension of fundamental consciousness.

Fundamental consciousness pervades every cell in our body. According to Hindu metaphysics, energy is a contraction, or condensation, of consciousness. Physical matter is a contraction, or condensation, of energy. Thus, in this system, all life is basically consciousness, and all matter is pervaded by consciousness and energy. We can also say that matter is organized by the consciousness that pervades it, in every atom or every cell.

If we now look at the human body in the light of this system, we will see that in every cell we will find consciousness and energy. We can therefore speculate that memory, as an aspect of consciousness, pervades every cell in the body. A memory of a particular moment in time will involve, and record, our entire being at that moment, including the energetic and physical levels of our being. This is why, when a memory becomes a bound pattern in the body, the binding contains the mental, energetic, and physical levels of our being.

An interesting question arises about the relationship between fundamental consciousness and our fragmented, bound consciousness. Eastern spiritual literature says that fundamental consciousness is really our own ordinary mind, but clearly perceived. Fundamental consciousness is our mind in its unbound, unmodified condition. Yet this same literature says that fundamental consciousness is never altered, has "never moved from the beginning." Then what is it that becomes contracted in our bound fragments and what is it that gradually realizes fundamental consciousness?

According to the Eastern teachings, there is a level of consciousness that becomes fragmented (or imprinted) while fundamental consciousness does not. This has been called the causal level of consciousness. Hindu metaphysics speaks of the causal level as a sheath or covering that obscures our recognition of fundamental consciousness.

As we release our bound patterns, the causal level becomes one with fundamental consciousness; it realizes fundamental consciousness. The actual feeling of this process, judging from my own experience, is that as we let go of our binding, our consciousness returns, like a released rubber band, into the vertical core of the body, expanding the experience of pervasive space (fundamental consciousness). The Hindu guru Sathya Sai Baba has said that enlightenment is when two aspects of the mind touch, apparently meaning the causal level and fundamental consciousness. Esoteric Christianity also refers to merging one's own mind in the mind of God.

The causal level of consciousness and fundamental consciousness are basically the same. It is only from the viewpoint of our bound fragments, our false self, that there is any kind of consciousness other than fundamental consciousness. But we should not infer from this that the fragmented false self can be disregarded because it is "unreal." For, as we have seen, our own true body, energy, and consciousness are bound in it. We must recover our bound self in order to become whole in the realization of fundamental consciousness.

Another important question is why some memories become bound in our body while others do not. Reich called the bound memories "pathogenic." Other writers have called them "unmetabolizable," using a digestive metaphor to describe this curious phenomenon in which some memories are literally stuck in our organism. Through careful observation of myself and my clients, I have arrived at the following "working" answer to this question.

I begin with the hypothesis that the newborn baby is at least relatively undefended. It may be, as Eastern theory contends, that we are born with the imprints of past lives. Perhaps our new body conforms to the defensive contractions in the subtle body that has traveled with us from the past. Or we (and I think this is quite likely) may have already been imprinted with some of the defensive pattern of our parents, either encoded into the sperm and ovum of our conception, or transmitted in the intermingling of our parents' fields of consciousness as we lay unguarded in the womb. But we can safely say that the baby is at least relatively undefended.

To be undefended means to be entirely available for experience. We can therefore speculate that the infant, within his limited sphere of budding perceptual and cognitive faculties, experiences the sensation, emotion, and awareness of each moment throughout his entire organism. He experiences both the inner and outer circumstances of each moment clearly and directly, without distortion. And although, as Daniel Stern's careful studies of infants have shown, he may know his own self from the selves and objects around him, he nevertheless experiences his own self and the environment as a single, unified field—that is, without rigid fragmentation between self and other.

However, from birth, and probably from as early as the prenatal months and during the birth process itself, many events occur which cannot be tolerated by the undefended child. These are the events that have been called "unmetabolizable." They are either too painful, e.g., food or affection deprivation; too frightening, e.g., a loving face transforming into a grimace of anger; too stimulating, e.g., loud sounds; or, as the child becomes more cognizant, too confusing, as in being told that one is loved while actually feeling smothered or shamed. Many of the intolerable events of early childhood are quite subtle, such as one's gaze not being directly met, one's love not being clearly matched, or one's feelings or needs being misread, so that the child feels out of sync with his environment. It is easy to see that no parent, no matter how well-intentioned, can provide a completely metabolizable life for a child.

The child recoils against the intolerable events—he cannot be entirely available for them. It is in this recoiling, this withdrawing of availability, this protective diminishing of experience that he begins to bind his consciousness, energy, and body. He begins to form fragments of bound life that are cut off from the rest of his consciousness. These bound fragments are in the shapes of our recoils from life, as well as in the shapes of our compensatory attitudes. Although they may produce an obvious postural change (such as stooping, or scoliosis), they are usually barely detectable densities hidden within the body. And as I have said, most defensive movements must be repeated over time, except in cases of severe or very early trauma, before they become bound in the tissues of the body.

In this way, the moments of our life that were too intolerable to experience fully are actually preserved in our field of consciousness, energy, and body. The body, energy, and mind in these fragments are literally tied up in the past, and are no longer available to function in the present. In other words, the defended child, and adult, is no longer entirely available for experience. All of his subsequent experience will be limited by the bound fragments in his body. There will be gaps in all his experience, where his awareness, emotion, and sensation are closed to life.

Here is an example of how this happens. An eighteen-month-old child is sitting in her high chair, being fed by her mother. She is not hungry and refuses the food, holding her mouth tightly shut to keep out the spoon. Her mother loses patience, becomes angry, and forces the spoon into the child's mouth, while threatening the child with punishment if she does not eat.

In this event a combination of intrusive, angering, and frightening circumstances overwhelms the child. She tenses her lips, mouth, and esophagus, as well as other parts of her body where she is experiencing anger, fear, and nausea. If this scene occurs repeatedly, this tension will become static and bound in her body. It will contain, for the rest of the person's life, unless some type of healing intervenes, the memory of the forced feeding, along with the anger, fear, and nausea she felt at the time.

The emotional content and the eighteen-month-old mentality

bound in her body will color all of her future experience, particularly in "trigger" situations involving eating, or taking in of nurture. The bound feelings and mentality will hang like a distorting veil, a "dream" between herself and her experience. If many of this sort of event have occurred in her childhood, she may feel as an adult that life has an inexplicable undertone of scariness and intrusiveness. In circumstances where there is a possibility of nurture, she may respond with the same rage and fear of being overpowered that she felt as an eighteen-month-old child. She will also build a belief system and a complex of secondary defenses around her limited and distorted experience. She may, for example, decide that she will never be nurtured in a way that meets her true needs and avoid intimacy, or that she is basically bad for causing her mother's anger (for having needs), or she may make an extreme effort to control her own intake of food, resulting in compulsive overeating or anorexia.

Most methods of psychotherapy treat only the secondary complex of beliefs and defenses. The limitation of this approach is that we may make changes in our beliefs or behavior without releasing the childhood emotions and mentality bound in our body. We will then continue to be haunted by the painful events of our childhood. We are literally trapped in a distorted, contracted relationship with the world as long as our childhood memories are bound in our body. And this binding will continue to impede our access to the vertical core of the body, and the realization of fundamental consciousness.

Releasing Emotional Pain from the Causal Body

There are many ways to facilitate the release of our bound memories. Any method that penetrates into the physical or energetic levels of the binding, or that helps people relax and loosen their grip on themselves, will help the release. However, I have found that the release is often only temporary unless the mental (causal) level of consciousness in the bound fragment is contacted. For example, people who are Rolfed often report that within a few months, the old tensions in their bodies have returned. This is because consciousness is basic to, and pervades and organizes the energetic and physical levels of our being.

It is the causal level of consciousness that organized the contraction of our energy and body. That same consciousness, if we can connect to it with our present-day consciousness, can let go of the contraction. Also, consciousness is fundamentally unbroken—it is the basis of our wholeness. When we contact the dimension of consciousness within our bound fragments, we contact our dimension of wholeness. This is the most direct, effective way of returning, or reconnecting, the bound fragments to the wholeness of our consciousness. This heals our fragmentation at the root.

To contact the dimension of consciousness in our bound fragments, we need to penetrate deeply and subtly into our binding, beyond the levels of energy and physical body. Here are two methods of achieving this deep, subtle contact.

EXERCISE 6   *Releasing the Bound Fragments*

Mentally locate the center of your head, between your ears and between your face and the back of your head, as described in exercise 3 in the last chapter. Feel that you are inside the center of your head.

From the center of your head, locate an area of tension in your body. By finding the tension from the center of your head, you are finding the core level, the level of fundamental consciousness, inside the tension. You are finding the level of the tension that has the same subtle quality as the center of your head.

Hold your focus steady in this way, breathing smoothly and evenly through your nose. Keeping this subtle focus, attune yourself to the emotional level of the tension. Keep breathing evenly. You may feel the emotion move towards release.

The release can occur as tears, or more subtly as vibration, the movement of energy (emotion is energy). This emotional vibration will dissipate as it moves out of your body. You may also experience a memory of a specific event or events in your childhood (rarely, binding occurs from adult trauma as well). And you may feel the quality or age of your childhood consciousness. Not all tensions in the body are bound memories. Tension can be purely physical, caused by injury or structural imbalance. Physical tensions can also be released in this way, by contacting the dimension of fundamental consciousness inside the tension, from the center of your head.

EXERCISE 7 *Releasing Bound Attitudes*

This second method can be used once you have discovered a habitual or bound attitude in your body, such as cringing, defiance, hypervigilance, and so on.

Let your body move into the bound attitude. Really experience yourself in this attitude. You may find that parts of your body that you did not know were involved in the attitude move into the pattern of tension. Because the whole body is connected through the fascia, our bound patterns often involve a line of tension throughout our whole body.

When you can feel the whole pattern of tension, try to attune to the consciousness that is holding the tension. Originally all of our binding was volitional, even though unconscious. The same part of your childhood mind that organized the contraction in your body is still preserved in the contraction. Try to experience the childhood mind that is holding the attitude that you experience in your body. You may experience the age that you were when you first formed this pattern. You may also experience the emotional content of the pattern.

As that childhood consciousness, you will be able to feel and discharge the bound emotion. Again, the emotional release may occur as tears, or as the movement of energy through and out of your body. The emotion will have the quality of your age when it was bound in your body. For example, the rage of a two-year-old has a different quality than rage of a six-year-old, or the rage of an adult. You will also be able, as the childhood consciousness, to let go of the physical tension, as simply as you can relax your hand after making a fist. This is not a method of regression in the usual sense of experiencing oneself entirely as a child. *Our present-day consciousness remains alert and witnesses the fragmented part of our consciousness, energy, and body that is bound in the childhood memory.*

Releasing the causal level of consciousness allows us to realize fundamental consciousness. Contacting the causal level of consciousness within the bound fragments in our body is the most precise, direct, thorough method of releasing our binding. The sensitivity and self-attunement necessary for this work gradually develops as we free more of the causal level of consciousness and access more fundamental consciousness.

Once we are living in the dimension of fundamental consciousness, we can perceive our binding as densities in the empty, unified space of fundamental consciousness. (Some people perceive the binding as areas of darkness in the space of fundamental consciousness.) It then becomes much easier to penetrate the contracted causal mind within these densities and reconnect it with the wholeness of fundamental consciousness. As the subtle structures or patterns gradually release, we experience the space of our consciousness as increasingly empty and unbroken. One man said that it was as if veils had dropped away, so that there was nothing in the way between himself and other people or objects. This is the direct experience of life that is one of the signs of enlightenment.

When we can clearly perceive that our childhood pain is held in the causal level of our consciousness, and can be freed from it as methodically as removing a splinter from our finger, it becomes obvious that we can never incur irreparable psychological damage. This is a crucial discovery for people who have sustained deep or very early childhood trauma, or who were born into an environment of pervasive, constant emotional pain. These people often feel permanently injured, or that they have always been in a state of psychological pain. For example, people who are chronically depressed will often report that their depression feels like their true nature, or that it feels "physical." Prolonged or severe psychological suffering does affect our chemistry and our whole physical well-being. Our bound pain greatly diminishes our energy system, which in turn diminishes our physiological functioning. When psychological pain has become a biological condition, the severity and the duration of its existence will influence how easily it can be healed.

Chronic psychological pain is no one's true nature. When a person is able to reach the dimension of fundamental consciousness, even deep-rooted or pervasive pain can be expunged from the body, and the energetic and physical functioning returned to health. For most people, this requires skillful, consistent psychological and spiritual work.

A few years ago I worked with a woman who had endured such severe sexual abuse that she was unable to have an intimate relationship. She could not talk or think about the abuse without an overwhelming feeling of shame and nausea. She told me that she felt there was something essentially dark and "rotted out" about her, and she was sure that she could never rid herself of this feeling. But over a three-year period, she was gradually able to attune to the clear open space of fundamental consciousness pervading her body. She was then able to feel that even the rotted out sensation was simply lodged in the space like a veil, as were the sharp splinters of terror and the burning pockets of rage that she encountered in the process of getting well. As the years passed I watched her regain her essential qualities—courage and power in her belly, tenderness in her heart, and what she called "sweetness" in her skin and sexual organs. Finally she told me that she perceived the inside of her body as "made of light."

I am not saying that we no longer feel any emotional pain, as we release the causal level of consciousness. It is our childhood pain, and the distortion of our present-day experience which gradually diminishes. In fact, as we release the bound energy of our past grief, anger, and fear, we gain emotional depth and fluidity in response to the current events in our life. We feel our emotions deeply, but we experience them as appropriate and temporal movements, passing through the unchanging ground of our fundamental consciousness.

As we mature, we begin to experience life from one, unified perspective, rather than from the many perspectives of our fragmented, bound consciousness. We grow towards wholeness. And we discover that our individual wholeness is, at the same time, the wholeness of self and environment. This is the subject of the next chapter.

4

Distance and Intimacy: Disentangling from the Object

ONE OF THE BIGGEST challenges on the spiritual path is to be able to get up from one's meditation pillow and maintain one's realized state of consciousness out in the world. Our fragmented, defended state was primarily created in relationship with other people, and so it is these encounters with other members of our own species that seem to be most rattling to our emerging sense of unity with the world. In order to stabilize in fundamental consciousness, it is important to understand how our realization of this dimension affects the way we relate with other people.

We will see in this chapter that it is as we reach our greatest distance from other people, in terms of our psychological and physical perspective, that we achieve oneness with them. The poet Kabir said that detachment and love are the "twin streams of enlightenment." This means that individuation and transcendence, distance and intimacy, separation and oneness all occur at the same time as we realize fundamental consciousness.

The Spatial Nature of Personal Growth

Fundamental consciousness pervades our entire body and the entire universe. In this dimension we experience the continuity, the unity, of our self and the environment. As I explained in the last chapter, our realization of fundamental consciousness is diminished by defensive contractions in the causal level of consciousness that, over time, rigidify and bind the energetic and physical levels of our being. The contractions in the causal level of consciousness contract and fragment our experience of the basic unity of self and environment. In other words, when our realization of fundamental consciousness is contracted (as it is to some extent in everyone), our experience of the self-environment unity is contracted, because fundamental consciousness is the dimension of self-environment unity.

The limitation in our experience of the self-environment unity is a limitation in our sense of space. In this contracted space, our perspective is literally shortened, so that people and objects seem closer to us in space than they actually are. Recently, when I was teaching this at a workshop, a woman told me, "All my life I've been saying I need space." This is a very common human complaint. Existential writers describing the human condition pointed repeatedly to this sense of suffocation and entrapment. To the extent that we are holding painful memories and emotions in our body, we live in a space that is too small for us. We cannot move or breathe or feel or think with ease. It is not the body itself that is a prison for the spirit, as some religious writing has suggested, but only the binding of pain in the body that confines us. As the causal level of consciousness releases its binding, we experience a sense of expansion and freedom.

In addition to shrinking the space we live in, so that we feel "glommed on" to the environment, our bound pain also creates a rigid fragmentation, or barrier, between the individual and the environment. In our defended body we feel separate from the environment. Wherever we have bound pain in our body there are gaps in our consciousness, gaps in our experience. We "fill in" these gaps with imaginary experience—the projections of our old fears, aversions, beliefs, and unfulfilled needs onto our present life. We experience a world "out there" of shadows and threats that is cut off from a world "inside" of fear and longing. This is the illusion of separateness that the Buddhists regard as our basic confusion.

We are thus both enmeshed with and divided from our environment. And the direction of growth is a simultaneous process of disentanglement and connection. As we let go of our defenses and projections, we find ourselves in the same continuous space, the same field of pervasive consciousness as the environment. Both disentanglement and oneness occur as we shift from living at the defensive boundary between our self and the environment, to living in the vertical core of our self.

When we live at our defensive boundary, we communicate from our own surface to the surfaces of the people and things around us. For example, we experience our self in our face, rather than in the center of our head, and we are aware only of the face of the person with whom we interact. When we touch, we feel only the contact of skin. But when we live in the vertical core and inner space of our body, we meet other life through the continuity of our own and the other's inner depth and content. We experience qualities of the other person, the timbre and tone of the intelligence behind the face, the movement of response and the vibrant stillness of essential being inside the skin. We connect and resonate with the subtle aspects of fundamental consciousness—the ground of awareness, emotion, and sensation that pervades all of us. With my own awareness, I am aware of yours. With my emotional quality, I feel the emotional quality of your being. With my physical sensation, I sense your physical sensation. This is more than connection—it is communion, the oneness that is our true relationship with all other life. As I have said, this communion occurs when we have grown further away from the world, inward to our deepest perspective in the vertical core of our body. Our greatest contact with the world occurs across the unfolded distance, the true distance, of fundamental consciousness.

Individuation

Most psychologists speak of the goal of personal growth as individuation. In the fifties, Margaret Mahler formulated a sequence of early childhood growth phases that became the basis of the predominant view of psychological development today. She said that the newborn infant is in a psychological state of virtual fusion with his mother and environment. He proceeds, given sufficient care and stimulation, to become increasingly aware of himself and the mother as separate entities. In the process he passes through phases of symbiotic attachment to his mother, a "practicing" phase of increased mobility and autonomy, a rapprochement phase in which his focus shifts between attachment to his mother and his new-found autonomy, finally arriving at object constancy, at about age three. With the attainment of object constancy, he is able to be alone, apparently secure that his mother will return eventually, and that he can enjoy his own self without fear of abandonment.

Mahler called this sequence the separation-individuation process. It has withstood the test of time because in clinical practice, psychotherapists see so many people who seem "stuck" at one or more of these phases before object constancy. It seems that we are all, to some extent, struggling to disengage from our attachment to our parents and environment, and to achieve an individual identity. By individual identity I mean the ability to perceive the world directly with our own senses, to understand our experience with our own mind, to feel that we inhabit our own body, to be able to surrender to the spontaneity of our own creativity and sexual passion, and to know that to a great extent, we can create the life circumstances of our own choice. In the therapeutic setting we have come to recognize that the path towards this separate identity is fraught with taboos and obstacles of many kinds. It is a state of advanced psychological health and maturity. I can safely say that by age three, almost all of us have experienced some wound that will impede our progress towards this goal even as adults.

In the past few years, Mahler's theory of separation-individuation has been challenged, most notably by Daniel Stern, and by therapists developing theories of feminine psychology. Stern's strongest objection to the separation-individuation theory is that it emphasizes the child's increasing separation and seems to ignore his growing capacity for intimacy. He writes, "Attachment and separation, or engagement and disengagement, are inextricably related, opposite sides of the same coin. . . . The structure and function of engagement and disengagement are interlocked so that the developmental history of one must encompass the developmental history of the other, regardless of which phase of development the child is in. The beginnings of separation and individuation must be contemporaneous with the beginnings of attachment."

Stern's observations of infants have also led him to conclude that the infant never confuses himself with the environment, is never in a state of total fusion or symbiosis. He feels there is a "sense of emergent self from birth." However, he does view childhood development as an increasing awareness of self and other, physically, emotionally and verbally, which he calls an "acquisition of new senses of the self." Although he differs with the specific phases outlined by Mahler, and feels she places too little emphasis on the child's growing connectedness with others, he does seem to agree with her main thesis that the direction of human growth is towards increasing individuation, along with the capacity for intimacy.

The arguments of feminine psychology also center around the ignoring and implied undervaluing of the child's developing capacity for intimacy in Mahler's scheme. This apparent undervaluing is seen to result in an undervaluing of feminine behavior, which is typically more concerned with intimacy than separation. Carol Gilligan, quoting Nancy Chodorow, whose analysis of gender identity is based on the studies of Robert Stoller, says, "Female identity formation takes place in a context of ongoing relationship since 'mothers tend to experience their daughters as more like, and continuous with, themselves.' Correspondingly, girls, in identifying themselves as female, experience themselves as like their mothers, thus fusing the experience of attachment with the process of identity formation. In contrast, 'mothers experience their sons as a male opposite,' and boys, in defining themselves as masculine, separate their mothers from themselves, thus curtailing their 'primary love and sense of empathic tie.' Consequently, male development entails a 'more emphatic individuation and a more defensive firming of experienced ego boundaries.'"

Thus feminine psychology argues that separation-individuation theory is gender-biased, judging psychological maturity by standards that do not encompass the developmental history of women. My own view of this subject is that, although men and women encounter different relationships with their mother and father, and different cultural expectations with regard to separation and attachment, both (undefended) individuation and the capacity for intimacy must be considered the goals of personal maturity for both genders. It is the legacy, from one generation to another, of bound pain and fragmentation, augmented by the shared imagery and beliefs of our society, that has created the frustrating, conflicted relationship between women who crave intimacy and men who opt for distance. For any individual to be relatively whole and without conflict requires a balanced capacity for both oneness and separateness.

From birth, we are trying to become fully ourselves in the context of our love for our parents. If childhood development were solely a matter of separation, there would not be nearly the degree of conflict and pain, and binding of pain in our body, as there is in this delicate balancing act between our deepening self-awareness, and our intensifying love for our parents. It is almost always for love that we give up (bind) those parts of our self that do not meet our parents' acceptance. And it is almost always for the sake of autonomy that we close ourselves off from our parents' love, when that love does not include the recognition and sanction of our separate identity.

Mahler presents her separation-individuation sequence as the normal, natural phases of the developing infant and child. This implies that she believes, as I do, that there is a spontaneous unfolding towards individuation. However, I place individuation in the ranges of advanced personal maturity, rather than at age three, as Mahler does. Daniel Stern voices a similar concern when he writes, "Clinical issues that have been viewed as the developmental tasks for specific epochs of infancy are seen here as issues for the lifespan rather than as developmental phases of life, operating at essentially the same levels at all points in development." Just as the child's development of the capacity for love and for separation is "contemporaneous," the spiritually maturing adult discovers that unity with the cosmos and individuation develop simultaneously in the dimension of fundamental consciousness. The child's first inkling of intimacy and separation is the rudimentary form of the spiritual master's unconditional love and serene detachment.

For the adult, individuation is a progression from a state of being merged with other people to a state of increasing independence and capacity for love. The merged state is a dependence upon the responses of others in order to feel good, safe, strong, and complete. There is an inability to use one's own senses and understanding, or to perceive and think for oneself. There is a sense of never being truly alone with oneself, and not being able to experience one's own sensations, feelings, and thoughts clearly. Daniel Stern writes that in situations of uncertainty, infants will "look toward mother to read her face for its affective content, essentially to see what they should feel, to get a second appraisal to help resolve their uncertainty." This looking at others to see what one should feel remains in the adult who has not yet discovered his separate identity.

R.D. Laing writes, "If the individual does not feel himself to be autonomous this means that he can experience neither his separateness from, nor his relatedness to, the other in the usual way. A lack of sense of autonomy implies that one feels one's being bound up in the other, or that the other is bound up in oneself, in a sense that transgresses the actual possibilities within the structure of human relatedness. It means that a feeling that one is in a position of ontological dependency on the other (i.e., dependent on the other for one's very being), is substituted for a sense of relatedness and attachment to him based on genuine mutuality."

Some people defend against this incomplete, dependent feeling by withdrawing from contact with other people. They are afraid of being overwhelmed, or feeling consumed by others, because they have so little felt sense of their own existence. Others become "addicted" to love, searching desperately for anyone who will merge with them and help them feel alive.

Relating in Fundamental Consciousness

In my work as a Subtle Self Work teacher, I have discovered that the state of being bound up with other people can be observed in a person's placement of consciousness. I said earlier that before we realize fundamental consciousness, we relate to the surfaces of other life from the surface of our self. In fact, most people are not even on the surface of their body; they are in front of their body. By this I mean that they habitually relate to the world, and experience themselves, from the space in front of their body. When we live in the shortened space of the contracted self-environment unity, we experience the center of our being in front of our body, rather than in the core of our body. To be bound up in other people is to literally live outside of our own body and self.

Most people are not at all aware of their relational style. But if I sit opposite someone and meet them at the point in space between us where they are situating themselves, they do usually become aware of their position of consciousness in space. And they will often recognize the position of our contact as familiar, as the relational style that existed in their childhood family. For reasons I will describe shortly, almost everyone has some degree of displacement of consciousness away from the vertical core and inner space of their body. Some people live just a little in front of their body, and others are much further separated from their true center. Some people relate by projecting themselves entirely into the person they are relating to, as if they were truly merged with them. I do not mean that they focus inside the other person's body, but that the origin of their focus, *where they experience the world from*, is inside the other person's body. Much has been said about the subjective nature of our sense of time, how time seems sometimes slower or faster, depending upon our psychological state. In the sense that I am describing here, our experience of space, or distance, is also subjective and relative.

As I have said, when our psychological defenses hold us in the contracted self-environment unity, we feel both merged with and defended against the environment. When we contact another person from the space in front of our body, rather than from the vertical core of our body, we are limited in our perception of that person, and in our ability to interact. This is because the source of our awareness, love, power, and sexuality is in the core of our body. When our access to the core is blocked, we are less capable of truly perceiving or loving or being sexually aroused by another person. Further, our interaction is usually distorted by the childhood emotions and needs that are held in our body, that block our access to our core and contract our experience of space. This means that we are not relating directly to the person we are with, but to earlier people and situations that the present relationship reminds us of. It is only as our perspective deepens and we begin to experience our separate wholeness, that we are capable of true contact with another person, from the true center of our being.

There are several reasons why we live and relate to the world from the space in front of our body.

1. Although a young child is relatively undefended, so that his experience of the self-environment unity is not defensively contracted, he still lives in a smaller experience of space than the undefended adult. Although the child's experience can only be a matter of speculation for us, we may rely on the assessment of expert observers like Mahler and Stern that the child begins life with only a rudimentary awareness of himself and the environment, and grows gradually towards individuation and relational ability. If you recall your own early childhood memories, you may notice that they take place in a small sphere of interaction, that the world consisted of the environs of a playpen, for example, or an object directly in front of you. But if you remember yourself as an adolescent, you may notice that your memory occurs within a larger context, such as a whole room. There is a natural process of growth that expands our sense of space, to the extent that it is not impeded by psychological defense. Although many young children have spiritual experiences, such as leaving their body or premonition, this is different than the experience of one's consciousness pervading and encompassing a vast expansion of space, extending in all directions, as occurs in spiritual maturity.

Our psychological defenses—the binding of consciousness in our body—occurred mainly in childhood, in interaction with the environment. Thus, these childhood defenses maintain the child's immature, up-close spatial relationship with the world in our adult body. When an adult relates to us from this shortened perspective, it is recognizably childlike. The person's lack of self-possession or separateness makes him seem dependent and malleable in the same way children are. Also, the parts of our consciousness that are bound in our defenses are not available for the process of maturation inward to the vertical core of our body. They remain stuck in the past.

2. The binding of childhood memory and pain in our body blocks our access to the vertical core of the body, and the

realization of fundamental consciousness. The binding also prevents us from inhabiting the parts of our body where the memories and pain are held. We cannot inhabit—we cannot pervade with our fundamental consciousness—the parts of our body that are bound. When we are unable to inhabit our body, our sense of self is displaced to the outside of our body.

3. As children, we distort our behavior in a variety of ways in order to maintain our parents' love. In this process, many of us become hypervigilant to the emotional climate and expectations of the environment. This is particularly so if our parents are violent, or unpredictably shifting in their approval and disapproval. Our attention shifts away from self-experience and becomes overly focused on the world outside of ourselves.

For example, I worked with a woman who kept her diffusely focused eyes glued to my face during our sessions. The center of her being seemed to be just a few inches from my face, even though we were seated several feet from each other. When she began to experience her diffuse, projected consciousness, she remembered a recurrent scene in her childhood. She was trying to play with her wooden blocks, as her mother rushed frantically around her, doing housework. When she accessed the part of her consciousness that belonged to the young child, she was able to see her mother very clearly, and could feel the emotional pain that her mother was in. She associated this pain with the frequent conflicts between her parents that sometimes erupted into violence. She could also feel her own fear that if she "abandoned" her mother by concentrating on her blocks, something terrible might happen to her mother. Here we see how the maturity that Mahler called "object constancy" can be obstructed. This child was unable to be alone with her own activity because her mother's place in her life did not seem assured. As an adult she still "held on" to people with her eyes, and could still not risk concentrating on her own inner experience.

4. We can add to this list the pressure of the mass media and social convention to conform our behavior and appearance to that of our peers, to live as a particular idea of a person, rather than as our own self. Conforming to standard norms of physical beauty, material success, and moral choices diminishes our attunement to our own self, and imbalances our consciousness towards the outside world. This is noticeable, for example, in women who project and actually live in and relate from a static image of conventional beauty superimposed on their own face and body. Feeling themselves to be objects, they relate from a superficial, objectified position, cut off from subjective experience.

5. One of the primary reasons that we relate to other people and experience our self from the space outside of our body is that we learned this relational style from our parents. Our parents are the first people we interact with in our lives, and our subsequent relationships are based on the relational style we learned from them. Because our parents live in defended bodies themselves, they necessarily relate to us from outside of their bodies. We automatically match our parents' position of consciousness in order to be in contact with them, and to feel that we belong in the family.

The natural direction of personal growth is for our consciousness to penetrate inward towards the core of our body. But a parent who has not gone far towards individuation (and most people have not) often gives the young child subtle signs of disapproval as the child begins to grow inward. These signs are often involuntary, unconscious facial expressions or, also unconscious, emotional vibrations of abandonment or anger. For example, a mother puts her two-year-old son on her lap as she always does, but this time the child looks at her from further back in himself, with a little more than his usual clarity. Responding only to what seems like a lack of closeness, the mother pulls the boy closer to her face and wraps him tightly in her arms. She wants to maintain the relational distance that feels comfortable and affectionate to her. However, this action actually thwarts the new level of contact that the child was ready for. The parent may also convey a lack of recognition, as if the child has become a stranger, or a withdrawal of affection. The child receives the unspoken message that to relate in a way that does not mirror the parent's way of relating jeopardizes the bond of love between them. In my work with people to help them relate from the core of themselves, the majority have reported some sort of familial taboo against this spatial/relational expression of individuation. Even though we actually experience greater contact with each other from the greater distance of our core, the shift into greater distance evokes a sense of risk.

For example, one woman was able to experience that she was relating to me from somewhere in the space between us, but she was reluctant to change it. After struggling with it for some time, she finally admitted to me that she did not think I really wanted her to make the shift inward. When I assured her that I did, she expressed disbelief that quickly dissolved into tears. To shift her sense of self inward felt disloyal to her mother, with whom she had been very close. She felt that if she let go of her merged style of relating, her mother would be brokenhearted, and might not even survive. She also feared being in the world as an adult, without the superimposed projection of her relationship with her mother. She said that to be in the core of her body felt like "going it all alone."

Many people fear that they will lose contact with the outside world if they live in the core of themselves, or that they will be abandoned. They feel guilty for separating from the environment, or angrily defiant, as if the separation could only occur as an act of rebellion. Very often people tell me that it feels selfish to be in their core. Others fear that they will be more clearly seen and known by another person if they live in their core, and rejected for who they really are. Although I have seen these reactions numerous times, and experienced them myself, I am still amazed that to be inside one's own body and relate to the world from there, can seem so fraught with danger.

I have also often observed the difficulty of separation from the parents' point of view. For many people, the enmeshed intimacy they enjoy with their young child satisfies the needs of their own wounded childhood mentality. Old rejections and losses are finally soothed by the dependent, clinging, unconditional affection of the young child. When the child begins to outgrow the parent's state of enmeshment, the parent feels abandoned.

I worked with a woman who felt loved for the first time in her life when her baby was born. She bloomed during the first two years of her child's life, becoming more content and confident than she had ever been. But one day she came to our session very upset. During their cuddle time, which was her favorite part of the day, her daughter had refused to lie down next to her, preferring to play with her toys instead. When the woman insisted that the child lie down with her, the child threw a tantrum, and the mother became enraged and screamed at her. Her source of love and attention was no longer focused solely on her. As for her child, she learned that there was something naughty about separating from her mother. She probably noticed that this incident was in some way worse than those times she had been yelled at for spilling or breaking something. For besides the anger in her mother's voice and facial expression, there was also hurt, and the accusation of emotional betrayal.

When adults begin the process of accessing the core of their body and relating to the world from their core, they encounter both the childhood pain bound in their body and the taboo against growing inward and experiencing themselves as separate from their parents. Individuation is a gradual process of resolving and releasing the pain of our early relationships. But almost everyone reports that they are finally able to love their parents more when they have gained some psychological distance from them and given up their childhood wish for their parents to be different towards them. At the same time, they are able to better love the people in their present-day relationships as they are able to contact them across the true distance of fundamental consciousness.

EXERCISE 8 *Relating from the Subtle Core*

Here is an exercise from the Subtle Self Work to help you experience relating to other people from the vertical core of your body.

Sit facing another person.

Mentally find the center of your own head, between your ears and between your face and the back of your head. Feel that you inhabit the center of your head. Experience the quality (how it feels) inside the center of your head. Remember, you should be able to feel the bottom of your torso by being in the center of your head, or you are placed too high in your head.

Staying in the center of your head, look at your partner, and be aware of the amount of spatial distance between you. Look into your partner's eyes across this distance.

Try to experience that even though there is another person in front of you, you still feel private inside your head, as private as if you were alone in the woods, or in your own room. Experience the quality inside the center of your head, as you maintain eye contact with the person in front of you.

Staying in the center of your head, mentally find the center of your partner's head. *Do not leave the center of your own head to find the center of your partner's head.*

If people find this difficult at first, I stand next to them and have them find the center of my head, staying in the center of their own head, without looking at me. It is easier for most people to do this than to stay in the center of their own head when someone is directly in front of them.

Now find your heart center, on the level of your heart but in the center of your chest, and deep within the core of your body. Begin by feeling your private connection to your own heart center, and the love that is in your heart even when you are alone.

Staying in your heart center, make eye contact with your partner across the spatial distance between you.

Staying in your own heart center, and maintaining eye contact, mentally locate the heart center of your partner. Do not come out of your own heart center to connect with your partner, but subtly attune to your partner's heart center from your own.

Now find your pelvic center, a couple of inches below your navel, in the vertical core of your body.

Experience your private connection to your own pelvic center.

Staying in your pelvic center, make eye contact with your partner, still aware of the spatial distance between you.

Staying in your own pelvic center, mentally locate the pelvic center of your partner.

When we find another person's core from our own, there is an unmistakable sense of contact between us. This contact feels like a perfect resonance, for at root we are all the same "I." This is our true oneness in the dimension of fundamental consciousness. One woman compared this experience to the "buzz" she felt when she was singing with someone and exactly matched their tone. We can experience this resonance with another person through the entire core of our body.

There is also, in this core-to-core contact, an automatic exchange of energy between people which can be felt, as well as seen by a sensitive observer. On the level of the center of the head, the exchange feels like clarity, or intelligence. On the level of the heart, there is an exchange of love. Most people are surprised to discover that when they pull back into their own core, they experience a spontaneous exchange of love with another person. We are particularly used to going out of our body and self to express love, and to assure the other person that we love them. But this separation from our core actually diminishes our ability to love by cutting us off from the source of our love. On the level of the pelvic center, the exchange has the quality of power, animal warmth, and sensuality. The spontaneous exchange of sensuality is part of our normal connection with all people, regardless of gender, and with all forms of life.

When I work with couples, I have them attune to each other in this way from all seven chakras (from the Hindu yoga system) along the vertical core of the body. This deepens their contact with each other, and it also helps heal imbalances in their relationship, such as struggles over power and submission, or the giving and taking of love. A very common imbalance in intimate relationships is when one partner overfocuses on the other (this is popularly called "co-dependence") while the other partner withdraws. When couples practice relating to each other from the vertical core of their bodies, communication, caring, power, and sexual exchange become more balanced.

Even in intimate sexual contact, the merging that occurs between spiritually mature individuals does not eradicate self-possession. We are unified with our sexual partner in the dimension of fundamental consciousness, and our energy systems do interpenetrate and blend. But we have our most intense, and most releasing, contact if we each remain in the vertical core of our own body. In this type of contact, both partners' centers are stimulated and opened. In this way, sexuality, or any exchange with another person, can facilitate personal, spiritual growth. When partners consistently practice this core-to-core contact, intimacy become a very effective spiritual path.

The exercise just described is also an excellent diagnostic tool, as well as treatment, for many psychological problems, as it involves a person's ability to make contact with himself and his environment. Whatever wounding has occurred in a person's interaction with the environment since birth will be reflected in the limitations of his ability to relate core to core, across the true distance between himself and other people.

This was illustrated by a man who came to work with me because he felt a great loneliness but seemed unable to find a lasting relationship with a woman. He referred to himself as a lady's man, going from one woman to another, without ever finding someone he wanted to commit to. When he did this exercise, he was able to relate fairly well from the center of his head to mine, and quite well from his heart center. But he was not able to relate to me from the core of his pelvic center. He could only access his own body in front of the pelvic center, his focus could not penetrate into the core of his body on the level of his pelvis. Because he could not access his pelvic center, the space between us on that level appeared shortened, as if he were tied to me by a short rope. Although he was a mature successful man, when he tried to connect to me from this area of himself, he looked like a little boy. He had the expression of a helpless, dependent child. Gradually, he was able to feel this expression in himself and to remember feeling that way in relation to his mother. As he began to penetrate inward towards the vertical core of his pelvis, he was able to feel again the many conflicted emotions of his relationship with her, and the great obstacles she had created to keep him from separating from her. He felt anger, guilt, and the deep pity that he had felt for her as a child, that kept him bound to her. As he released (penetrated through) the binding in his body that had held these emotions hidden from him for so long, he was able to contact the core of his pelvis and relate to women from a mature distance, and to feel true intimacy with them.

When people are able to actually experience that they can connect to the world from their own core, they feel less susceptible to rejection and abandonment. They have a felt sense that they exist, and will go on existing even if the person providing them with love and acknowledgment is no longer there. Virtually all of us had to negotiate an economy of love and autonomy in interaction with our parents. To experience self-possession and intimacy at the same time is thus a significant breakthrough for everyone I've worked with. Many people have also said that in this new level of safety and balance in their connection with other people, they are able to feel an appreciation and reverence for human life that previously they had felt only for animal and plant life.

Understanding the spatial nature of personal growth gives us a new way to perceive and heal the boundary issues and the disassociation from ourselves that we all suffer to some extent in our defended relationship with life. Even people with more severe schizoid, borderline, and narcissistic problems, who have defended themselves by imagining the world to be all-me or all-other, can learn to integrate distance and intimacy when they experience the world from the vertical core of their body. Psychotherapists and spiritual teachers need to be able to recognize the shift in consciousness from the periphery of the body to the inner depth and core of the body that reflects the shift in perspective from entanglement and projection to individuation and connectedness.

We also need to be able to help people wrestle with the many taboos, familial and cultural, against continuing the inward path toward the realization of fundamental consciousness. Even if we are no longer in contact with our parents, the old threat of punishment for separation is still operative in our bound childhood mentality. And it is a terrible punishment that we imagine—estrangement, the cessation of love, the loss of belonging. Almost as potent is the fear of estrangement from our peers for separating from the static beliefs, behaviors, and goals of our social milieu. It takes courage to shift our loyalty from the stone tablets of tradition to our own judgment, which arises spontaneously in the dimension of fundamental consciousness. And it takes great courage to proceed on a path that is entirely invisible to all but a few.

We often experience a phase of painful aloneness as we separate from our family of origin and the standard imagery of our society. This phase is expressed in the philosophy of existentialism, in which the individual is seen as the sole point of reference. But aloneness is as illusory as attachment. We are not alone. We exist in a unified field with all other life. The paradox is that the more we realize our individual existence the more we experience that we are inextricably connected with the whole of life. We can relate to our community as caring and (relatively) free individuals, with the will and vision to work for change, as well as the detachment to live, without defensive boundaries, in the midst of the world's confusion.

Detachment

As we shift from the contracted space of our psychological binding to the expanded, unified space of fundamental consciousness, we begin to experience detachment. The teaching of detachment has been as misunderstood as the teaching of selflessness. Detachment does not mean a lack of responsiveness, interest, or passion. Our disentanglement from the projections and defenses of our past means that we have greater availability for present-day experience, greater depth and resilience in all the capacities of our being. We are able to be alone with our self, alone in our own body, and also alone with others, without the remembered voices of our early relationships.

Gradually we find that we can drop our agenda for getting our old needs satisfied, and our old wounds recompensed or revenged.

We have less need for people to act towards us in a particular way, or to manipulate our circumstances through denial, avoidance, aggression, or self-limitation. We are more able to let life happen, without anxiety about the outcome of events. The true meaning of detachment is this ability to allow our self and others to be just as we are, to let each moment of life—both our perceptions and responses—unfold spontaneously.

A few months ago I attended a lecture by a visiting Tibetan Buddhist teacher from Ladakh. A Buddhist teacher who lives here in the United States was translating for him, so they were sitting quite close to each other on the stage. I was struck by the relationship between these two men, but it took me a while to realize what seemed so unusual to me. Although there did not appear to be intimate friendship between them, there was also no defensiveness. They seemed to be receiving each other completely, without the usual guardedness, and without any trace of pulling back or pushing against each other. They were not trying to control each other, or themselves, or the audience in any way. Not only did they appear to be free of commercial strategy, or the need to keep us entertained and coming back for more, they seemed to be free of any predetermined rules of behavior. Although Tibetan culture is in many ways more formal than ours, more involved with protocol and hierarchy, these two spiritual teachers seemed unafraid that they would commit any social gaffe, and unconcerned that the audience might favor one more than the other. They were not observing or presenting themselves to us, but seemed completely at ease and open to our appraisal. Their freedom gave the audience the freedom to respond honestly and spontaneously.

Detachment is the experience that fundamental consciousness pervades our self and environment, and that whatever happens in our self and environment occurs without disturbing our attunement to the infinite stillness of this dimension. Even if we are profoundly moved by something, this movement occurs as a transitory pattern of vibration in the vast, empty, unbroken space of fundamental consciousness.

Thus detachment does not at all mean that we become zombies, aloof from the emotional richness of human life. Detachment is the full, direct experience of life at the same time as we experience the unchanging ground that pervades our life. Just as we can hear music most clearly when we are silent, the dynamic interplay of our reception and responses to life is experienced most clearly in the stillness of fundamental consciousness. Although we will not act on all our responses, for our judgment is also functioning freely, we will experience the full range and depth of our sensations, emotions, cognitions, and perceptions without interference or distortion.

There is a Zen story on this theme about an accomplished Zen master whose wife has just died. One of the master's students is alarmed to find his great teacher, who has given such inspiring talks on the impermanence of life, sobbing in his garden. "Why are you crying?" the student asks. "Because I am sad," answers the master.

Detachment is actually the freedom to cry at our losses, rage at those who oppress us, and feel fear when we are threatened. It is probably true that if we were completely enlightened, we would not experience any loss, oppression, or threat. But for the long duration of our progress towards complete enlightenment, our realization of fundamental consciousness is partial. In this partial realization, there continues to be a sense of I and other, at the same time that we experience the unity of I and other. It is very important to understand the nature of this partial realization, because we cannot progress in our enlightenment if we pretend to be further along, or in any way different, than we are at any particular moment. Many spiritual students get "stuck" trying to act detached when detachment is really a matter of letting life be just as it is. As I have said, our emotional responses gradually become less related to the projections of our childhood pain and more related to our present-day circumstances, as we continue in our realization of fundamental consciousness. Although we do not become less passionate in our responses to life, our passion loses the urgency of the bound "inner child" to be loved, and becomes the free flowing of our love, sexuality, and intelligence in relationship with the life around us.

Detachment requires trust that events will unfold in a way that is basically, or ultimately, beneficial to everyone involved. We can trust both other people and ourselves because we trust the underlying consciousness that contains us both. I will speak more about this "cosmic trust" in the last chapter. Here I will say that fundamental consciousness is a unified intelligence. It is the basis of the interpenetrating nature of the dreams and destinies of all forms of life. If we surrender to the spontaneity of ourselves and others, if we can let go of our fear and allow life to happen, we will be carried towards complete enlightenment. Detachment is the surrender of our resistance to this natural flow of life towards enlightenment.

EXERCISE 9   *Letting Life Go Through*

9A) Here is an exercise that I do with people to help them experience the unchanging, unbreakable nature of fundamental consciousness.

I ask the person to begin with exercise 1 from chapter 1: Experience that you are inside your whole body at once. Mentally find the space outside your body, the space in the room. Now experience that the space inside and outside your body is the same, continuous space; let it pervade you. Experience that the space pervading your body also pervades the other people and objects in the room. Experience that the space pervading your body also pervades the walls of the room.

I then tell the person that I have an imaginary red ball, about the size of a pea, and that I am going to gently toss the ball through the clear space of fundamental consciousness that pervades their body.

I toss the ball through the space over their right shoulder. Then over their left shoulder. Next, I toss the ball through the right side of their chest. Then through the left side of their chest. In this way, they can experience that even the substance of their body is permeable in the dimension of fundamental consciousness.

The tossing of the ball is not entirely imaginary because the movement of my hand creates a current of energy. Many people will flinch or subtly close their attunement to fundamental consciousness against this current. The exercise is practiced until the person can remain in the dimension of fundamental consciousness and allow the ball to pass through his or her body without flinching or closing.

This exercise can then be applied to daily life, allowing the various energies in the environment to pass through our attunement to fundamental consciousness, without flinching, recoiling, or shutting out experience. This allows us to receive and respond to life fully while remaining grounded in our fundamental being. It allows each moment to register and pass in the field of fundamental consciousness, without distortion. It also enables us to be in the presence of other people's pain and confusion without feeling threatened or overwhelmed.

9B) In another version of this exercise, I stand close to the person and create an emotional energy in their field of fundamental consciousness, such as anger or sadness, by making a sound that expresses that emotion. This is practiced until the person can allow the emotional current to pass through their attunement to fundamental consciousness, just as they allowed the imaginary ball to pass through, without flinching or closing against it. Many people will let the emotional current change their emotional state—they feel the emotion as if it were their own. They have lost attunement to the field of fundamental consciousness that pervades themselves and me. They have lost contact with themselves and become me. To feel my emotion as if it were their own is very different from having an emotional response to my emotion.

Many sensitive people report that they cannot tell, in their daily lives, if their emotional state is their own or if they have "taken on" the emotional state of people around them. These people are so disoriented by the many emotional states in the environment that they may begin to avoid social interaction. Or they may become martyrs to their sensitivity, making their own hearts and bodies a kind of communal arena. Techniques have been developed for sensitive people to protect themselves from the vibrations around them, but these techniques both limit our openness to experience and promote the illusion that the feelings of others can harm us in some way. The vibrations of others can only harm us if we ourselves close our consciousness against them. When we become stable in our realization of fundamental consciousness, we may feel another person's pain, and respond to it, but we will not feel another person's pain as our own.

In the same way that we need not fear the emotions of others, we can allow our own pain its full depth and movement in the unchanging stillness of fundamental consciousness. Our true nature can never be injured. We can therefore allow ourselves to be fully available for experience and our essential being will endure and become even more accessible to us.

Conclusion

In this chapter I have described the spatial nature of personal growth. Individuation is a process of growing inward towards the vertical core of our body, deepening our perspective so that we relate to the world across increasing distance. As we achieve this separation from the environment, we achieve oneness with the environment, because it is through the vertical core of our body that we attune to the pervasive, unified dimension of fundamental consciousness. We access the source, and thus the greatest potency, of our awareness, love, and sensation, in the vertical core of our body. This means that our oneness with the environment is rich with these essential qualities of our being.

We have also seen in this chapter that fundamental consciousness is a dimension of disentanglement from both our inner and outer experience of life. It is important to understand that we do not become unfeeling or unthinking zombies, nor does the outer world disappear with this disentanglement. The more disentangled we become, the more fully we pervade our experience, and this makes life richer, deeper, and more vivid.

5

The Body of Clear Space

THE REALIZATION of fundamental consciousness has a profound effect on the body. It produces a radical shift both in our experience of embodiment, and in the appearance and functioning of our body.

As fundamental consciousness, we pervade our whole body at once. Becoming completely enlightened is a long, gradual process. I believe that we cannot entirely pervade our body until we are completely enlightened. As we progress in our enlightenment, we gain increasing access to the inner depths of the body, to the cells that make up all aspects of our anatomy, including our nerves, blood, and the marrow within our bones. Gradually we also pervade the complex system of subtle channels that have not yet been charted by Western science.

But even with our initial realization of fundamental consciousness, we experience a shift from a fragmented sense of the body to a sense of wholeness. In the fragmented sense of the body, we can be conscious of our chest but not our legs, for example, or of our head but not our feet, in the same moment. As fundamental consciousness, we experience our whole body (all that we are capable of accessing) at once. (In other words, there may be parts of our pelvis, for example, that are too defended to be pervaded by fundamental consciousness, but we will still be able to include the rest of the pelvis in our total body experience.) Also, in the dimension of fundamental consciousness, we experience our body from the inside. Rather than being conscious *of* a part of our body, it feels as if our body is conscious of itself.

As fundamental consciousness, we experience no difference, no gap, between our consciousness (our self) and our body. Our body is part of our consciousness. It feels like our body is made of consciousness. And this consciousness is both permeable and substantial. We experience our body as empty space, and at the same time, it feels full and buoyant. There is also a quality in the realized body that is the essence of our aliveness. Many times I have seen people search for the right word to describe this new experience and finally come up with the word "human." When we pervade our body as fundamental consciousness, we feel more human.

In the dimension of fundamental consciousness, the body has the receptive and expressive capabilities of consciousness. We are able to receive each moment through the inner depths of our body. We experience that each moment occurs inside and outside of our body at the same time, without any gap between inner and outer experience. At the same time, the realized body expresses the many types and shades of human experience, not just in the voice or eyes, but through the whole depth of all its parts. For example, the Indian spiritual master Sathya Sai Baba once showed me the embodiment of patience. Without even changing his posture, he suddenly began to emanate, as if through every cell in his body, the quality of patience.

In the far reaches of enlightenment, the body becomes as permeable as pure consciousness. There have been many reports (for example, Yogananda in *Autobiography of a Yogi*) of spiritual masters who are able to move through walls, or put their hands through material objects. Just as, in the beginning of enlightenment, we can experience that our mind pervades the walls of a room, the advanced master can penetrate the wall with his whole body. Physical and mental have become the same.

To a sensitive observer, the body of fundamental consciousness looks smooth and unbroken, like a pebble that has been repeatedly washed by the sea. There is an appearance of luminosity and transparency. The wholeness of the body makes it more harmonious, and its movements fluid and light. In advanced spiritual masters, these qualities are extreme and easily seen. But even in people who have only begun to realize fundamental consciousness, these changes are visible.

Also, when a person realizes fundamental consciousness, the eyes and the whole body seem more permeable. We can look into the depths of a realized body and see the movement of feelings and sensations in that body. A more defended body looks flatter. Both the eyes and the rest of the body have an opaque quality—we cannot look into them easily.

It is exactly the same with touch. If we touch a more defended body, there is no sense of depth beneath our hand. But if we touch a body that is pervaded by fundamental consciousness, we can feel the whole inside of that person at once, without changing the position of our hand.

The way we experience our self is also flatter in a more defended body. We cannot feel or sense deeply, and this makes life seem unreal, or meaningless. As we begin to become aware of our self in our defended body, we often feel confined and uncomfortable. Since our breath is contracted along with the rest of our body, we may feel that we are almost suffocating. As we release our defenses, our experience of life becomes fuller and richer. We begin to feel at ease and "at home" in our body. As fundamental consciousness, we register all of our sensations, emotions, perceptions, and cognitions at once, in each moment.

Misconceptions about the Body and Enlightenment

Many spiritual traditions ignore the body, or if they mention it, they say things that are easily misinterpreted, like "the body drops away." What drops away in enlightenment is the experience of dichotomy between the body and consciousness. The objectified body "drops away." In enlightenment, we drop into the body. We settle into the body's dimension of fundamental consciousness.

When spiritual traditions do not mention the body, the students often wind up meditating on the space outside, or above, the body. This prevents them from accessing the vertical core of the body, or allows them to access only the top of the vertical core, severely limiting their realization of fundamental consciousness. Enlightenment occurs in the body. It is as much a transformation of the body as it is anything else.

Another teaching that causes confusion about the body is the Hindu Vedantic technique for arriving at fundamental consciousness. The student of Vedanta is taught to say, "I am not my body, I am not my energy, I am not my thoughts." In this way, he recognizes that he is nothing that he can point to; rather, he is that which does the pointing—the ground itself, pure consciousness. Becoming enlightened shifts our identity from the muscular surface of the body to the most subtle dimension of consciousness pervading the body, the dimension of pure being. If the Vedantic technique is understood correctly, the student will recognize that although he is not only his body, he is pervading his body.

Once I worked with a man who had been a student of Vedanta for many years. He was an accomplished scientist in his mid-sixties. He had a teacher in India who had told him that all he had to do was to understand that his true identity was the non-dual, all-pervasive Self, and he would be completely enlightened. This intelligent, thoughtful man had spent the past twenty years reading Vedantic literature and trying very hard to understand his true identity. But he felt no more enlightened than when he had first begun.

Working with him, it was obvious that he had a great deal of difficulty breathing. His chest was tight with held grief and his whole body moved up and down as he breathed. It took intense effort for him to contact the inner space of his body and remain aware of the room around him at the same time. Although he knew exactly what the Vedanta said about the true Self, he was far from the subtle experience of non-duality. We have to actually let go of the body with our mind in order to live in the disentangled space of fundamental consciousness. This is not just a matter of understanding—it must involve self-attunement and the release of defensive rigidities in the body which block self-attunement.

Another misconception is the popular notion, promoted by some Western psychotherapies, that we need to get "out of our head and into our body." This much-used phrase implies that the function of the head is only to produce abstractions and concepts that keep us from experiencing life directly. The word "head" is used to describe static mental ideation. This teaching leads people to hold still or "fog out" their mental faculties, or to work on inhabiting their whole body except for their head. This elimination of the head from our experience of self intensifies our fragmentation.

It is crucial to our personal growth that we inhabit our head along with the rest of our body. The body of fundamental consciousness is a body without static attitudes and beliefs; it is the body of the true self. But the true self does have a head. As fundamental consciousness, we are still able to recognize, contemplate, and understand our experience. Just as we are able to sense and feel more deeply in the dimension of fundamental consciousness, we are also able to think more clearly. The aspect of awareness that we attune to through the upper third of the vertical core of the body is an essential aspect of fundamental consciousness, along with the aspects of emotion and physical sensation.

Transformation of the Body—the Senses

The body is the instrument of our perception. As our body becomes more subtle, our perception becomes more subtle, too. In the same way that we perceive our own form as made of consciousness, we perceive that the other forms in our environment are also made of consciousness. We see that the transparency and permeability of our own being is equally true of the life and objects around us.

Enlightenment is thus a refinement of all our senses. It is a seeing through, and a hearing, smelling, and touching through life—that is, through the dimensions of physical matter, energy, and consciousness. We are able to see the energy in the environment as movement, radiance, and color; to hear it as a subtle buzzing sound; and to touch it as vibration and liveliness. We perceive fundamental consciousness in the environment as empty space, pervading everything. And we perceive these three dimensions: physical matter, energy, and consciousness, all at the same time.

When we realize fundamental consciousness, we experience that instead of five separate senses, we now have one unified medium of perception. As fundamental consciousness, we reflect all sensory stimuli at once. We do not have to look in order to see, or to listen in order to hear. The clear space of fundamental consciousness pervades all of our sense organs. All of the sights, sounds, tastes, smells, and textures of each moment occur simultaneously, without any effort on our part.

A defensive constriction anywhere in the our body diminishes our realization of fundamental consciousness, and limits the subtlety of our perception in general. But many of our defenses are direct constrictions of the senses. As children, we particularly bind our organs of perception to minimize our experience of painful circumstances. For example, we may bind our visual apparatus so that we do not see the angry look on our parent's face. Or we may bind the anatomy of our hearing so that we do not hear the sorrowful tone in our parent's voice. Also, many children are discouraged from using their senses fully by adults who feel anxious or ashamed when perceived too clearly, or by adults who are themselves in denial of an aspect of reality, such as a drinking problem, or a problem in their marriage. The child is then told, directly or indirectly, that his perception is inaccurate. He may even be made to understand that his perception is potentially damaging to the well-being of the family. The child then limits his perception to accommodate the adult's version of reality.

As we release our defenses, our senses become clearer. We begin to perceive a more vivid world. We also become sensitive to balance, or harmony, in the world. Because our perception is functioning in a more global way, pervading and reflecting all the sensory stimuli in our range of consciousness in each moment, we become more attuned to the relationship between sensory stimuli. For example, we hear the sounds of the birds singing at the same time, and within the same spatial field of consciousness, as we hear the sound of our neighbors laughing, and the sound of the distant lawnmower, and the sound of nearby footsteps on a gravel road. We enter the artist's realm of intervals and counterpoints. Like the artist, we perceive the unity and underlying wholeness of each moment's various shapes, tones, timbres, and textures.

Our senses also reflect the fragmentation of our consciousness, and where we are open or defended in our body. For example, if we live mostly in the top of our body, in the dimension of awareness, we will see with mostly the top portion of our eyes. People who are intellectually, but not emotionally or sensually developed, will have this type of visual fragmentation. This limits the visual impression that is received. If we see with only the top portion of our eyes, we will not be sensitive to the emotional depth or sensual texture of the objects or people we see. If we live mostly in the bottom of our body, in the dimension of physical sensation, we will see with mostly the bottom portion of our eyes. If we live mostly in the emotional dimension, we will see mostly with a narrow band in the middle of our eyes. As we realize fundamental consciousness, we see with the whole body and mind. We can only see the whole picture if we see with our whole eyes. The same is true for all of our senses.

EXERCISE 10   *Seeing with the Whole Eye*

Look at an object in front of you.

Try to see it with only the top portion of your eyes.

Try to see it with only the middle portion of your eyes.

Try to see it with only the bottom portion of your eyes.

Notice how your visual placement changes how you perceive the object. Also notice how the shifts in your visual placement change where you experience yourself in your body.

Now feel that you are inside your whole body all at once. Perceive the object with your whole eyes. Experience that you are seeing the object with your whole body and mind.

You can also observe the visual placement of the people around you. The part of their eyes that they are looking through will tell you where they most experience themselves in their body. Often when two people have difficulty making contact with each other, it is because they are looking at each other from different portions of their eyes—they literally do not see eye to eye.

EXERCISE 11   *Touching with Your Whole Self*

Our fragmentation or wholeness effects all of our senses. We can see, hear, touch, smell, and taste with our whole body and mind. Here is an exercise to help you experience this in the sense of touch.

Put your hand on the surface of an object or person.

Touch it with only your dimension of awareness.

Touch it with your emotional dimension.

Touch it with your dimension of physical sensation.

Now touch it with all three dimensions at once, with your whole being.

For most people, it is a new, and very satisfying experience to touch, or be touched, so completely.

Energy

Energy is the dynamic aspect of our being, moving through the vast stillness of fundamental consciousness. Our energy system is a complex circulatory system of varying vibrations from gross to subtle. As we realize fundamental consciousness, this circulation is able to move more freely through our organism.

The different subtleties of energy are associated with diverse functions. For example, there is energy associated with organ and other physiological functioning, as described in Chinese and Japanese medicine. There is energy associated with discharging of emotions, as discussed by Wilhem Reich and his students, such as Alexander Lowen and John Pierrakos. As we access the vertical core of the body, we experience our most subtle, most powerful energy called *kundalini* in Hindu yoga. Our energy is constantly changing in response to stimuli, to our moods, health, and activity. This movement occurs in the stillness of fundamental consciousness, without ever changing or disturbing it.

Breath

As we realize fundamental consciousness, we experience a profound change in the way we breathe. Our breath becomes more refined, smoother and quieter, with a subtle electrical quality. The breath feels as if it is half-breath, half-mind. We also experience that the breath reaches everywhere in our body, that it nourishes all of our cells.

Another change that occurs as we begin to inhabit our body fully is that we bring the breath in and out through the center of our nostrils. If we live primarily in the upper third of our body, in the dimension of awareness, we will bring the breath in too close to the tip of our nose. If we live primarily in the bottom third of our body, in the dimension of sensation, we will bring the breath in too close to our upper lip. If you take a moment to observe your own breathing, you will see that the part of the nostril you breathe through is related to where you are in your body. You may also find that breathing in and out through the center of your nostrils makes breathing much easier.

EXERCISE 12 *Refining the Breath*

Here is an exercise to make your breathing easier and more subtle.

Mentally find the center of your head. Again, the center of the head is between your ears, between your face and the back of your head.

Bring the breath in through the center of the opening of each nostril. Bring the breath all the way into the center of your head on the inhale, and then exhale through the centers of your nostrils. Let the breath be fine and silent—half-breath, half-mind —so that it can penetrate through your head into the center.

Now bring the breath in through the centers of your nostrils, into the center of your head and down the length of your throat towards your upper chest. On the exhale, bring the breath back up into the center of your head and out your nostrils. Try to actually feel (not visualize) the breath as it moves through you.

Next, bring the breath in through the centers of your nostrils, into the center of your head, down your throat and into your lungs, filling the lungs with breath. On your exhale, bring the breath back up into the center of your head and out your nostrils.

Bring the breath in through the centers of your nostrils, into the center of your head, down your throat, into your lungs, and then into your whole body. Feel that the breath reaches every cell in every part of your body. On the exhale, bring the breath back to the center of your head and out your nostrils.

Most important in this exercise is that the breath passes through the center of your head on both the inhale and the exhale. When the breath passes through the center of the head, it becomes refined by integrating with our most subtle energy in the vertical core of the body. In that refined condition, it can reach everywhere in the body. As you practice, let the breath be smooth and effortless.

The breath is one of the most obvious bridges between inner and outer experience. Every defensive binding in the body diminishes our ability to breathe freely and easily. Neither our consciousness nor our breath have access to the rigid, defended parts of our body. Further, just as with our senses, most of us have directly defended our breath so as not to feel our own pain or take in the painful emotions in our childhood environment.

It can take some coaxing to convince ourselves as adults to breathe the air in our current environment. But we cannot be present in ourselves unless we breathe the air that is here now. This process of coming into the present with our breath is an important component of personal growth. It is part of learning to feel safe, to open to and directly experience our oneness with the environment.

As we begin to live in the vertical core of the body, and in the dimension of fundamental consciousness, we experience that our breath is actually initiated in the whole vertical core, rather than at our nostrils. There is a sense that our breath and consciousness are breathing together in the vertical core of the body. This is because our breath has become so subtle that it is integrated with our most subtle energy, which is the interface between consciousness and energy. This subtle breath has a mental quality to it—it feels as though our mind is breathing in the vertical core of our body. To be able to live in the dimension of fundamental consciousness all the time, we need to breathe with the vertical core of the body. Exercise 3 in chapter 2 will help you initiate the breath from the vertical core of the body.

Speech

Many people have told me that it is most difficult for them to remain in the dimension of fundamental consciousness when they are speaking. The anxiety that many people have about verbal expression creates an automatic defensive contraction in the throat in preparation for speech that blocks attunement to fundamental consciousness. We can maintain attunement to fundamental consciousness while speaking by consciously inhabiting our neck, vocal mechanism, and the subtle channel in the vertical core of the neck. The voice becomes more authentically expressive when we inhabit our vocal anatomy, making it easier to verbalize our true thoughts and feelings. We also feel safer when we inhabit our body because we have a felt sense of our own substance. It is less likely that we will feel the need to defend our voice if we experience the substance and quality of our being while we are speaking, or about to speak.

The two most common defenses in preparation for speech are contracting downward in the neck, towards the chest, and displacing the consciousness upward from the neck into the head. It is helpful in both cases to consciously inhabit the upper chest, as well as the neck. If we experience that we are "sitting in our heart" while we speak, it will keep us from leaping up into our head, or obstructing the flow of breath from our lungs to our larynx.

Gravity and Balance

Another important shift that occurs in our body as we realize fundamental consciousness is our relationship with gravity. Gravity is an essential component of the spontaneous process of personal growth. In this chapter I will describe how the shift in our relationship with gravity affects the body. In the next chapter, I will discuss this shift in terms of our relationship with the cosmos.

Before we realize fundamental consciousness, we experience our body as a solid mass of physical matter, rigidly separate from the environment. We therefore experience gravity as a force outside of our body that pulls us towards the ground, as we struggle to remain upright. This struggle against gravity results in chronically held muscles, which limit our movement and cause pain and exhaustion.

Gravity is part of our energy system, just as it is part of the energy, or movement, system of the universe. When we experience our self and our body as fundamental consciousness, rather than as material solidity, we are able to experience that the movement of gravity passes through our body and being, through the clear, open space of fundamental consciousness. This movement is both inside and outside of our individual body. It is part of our oneness with the environment and the cosmos.

Our openness to the movement of gravity determines our degree of balance. To the extent that we are not open (defended), gravity will not be able to penetrate through our body evenly, and we will be off-balance. All life is off-balance to some extent. As we become open to life, gravity moves through the inner depths of our body, settling our whole being towards the ground in a balanced way. This is the same as saying that we are able to relax. We are able to release our grasp on our body, energy, and mind and open deeply and evenly to the movement of gravity through our being. As we become more balanced, we begin to experience our continuity with the Earth, in the dimension of fundamental consciousness. We experience that fundamental consciousness pervades our body and the Earth without any gaps. Thus balance brings us into our oneness with the planet.

An interesting thing happens as we settle our weight towards the ground. We experience not only the downward current of gravity, but also an upward current that comes up from the ground and rises through the inner depths of the body. This upward current makes the body light and buoyant. It supports us. There is actually no need for us to struggle to stay upright. The more we settle to the ground, the more we become relaxed and open, the more we experience this upward accompaniment to the force of gravity. I call this upward current the upward movement of gravity because it occurs as a direct result of our settling downward.

Gravity is part of our spontaneous realization process. Over time, the downward and upward current deepens in our body, finally penetrating and awakening consciousness in the vertical core of the body. As the movement of gravity deepens towards the core, it penetrates and opens the bound tissues in our body, releasing to consciousness our repressed memories and emotions. Thus gravity is at least partly responsible for the spontaneous surfacing of repressed material that is noticed in psychotherapy, in dreams, and through other means that I will describe in the next chapter.

Once we have begun to realize fundamental consciousness, we can observe and feel this deepening of the movement of gravity in our body. The challenge is to allow this movement to occur—not to interfere with it. Our growth depends upon our letting go of our defensive grasp on our self. We grow by surrendering to gravity.

EXERCISE 13   *Opening to Gravity*

Here is an exercise to help you experience the upward movement of gravity in your body. This current is extremely subtle and may take some practice to experience.

Stand, without your shoes, on a level floor.

Feel that you are inside your whole body all at once, including your feet.

Feel that there is no separation between you and the floor. Feel the continuity of yourself and the floor.

Mentally find the centers of the soles of your heels.

Balance your awareness of these two points—find them both at exactly the same time.

Open these centers to the current that rises upward from the ground. This current rises through your whole feet, but it enters most easily through the centers of the soles of your heels.

Do not force the current upward, but subtly attune to its spontaneous movement. Allow the current to rise upward through the inside of your whole body.

The body of fundamental consciousness is light and buoyant because of the upward movement of gravity. But it is also relaxed and settled to the ground, because of gravity's downward force. Some people experience themselves as shorter, or heavier, as they realize fundamental consciousness because they feel closer to the ground. For people whose placement of consciousness has been mostly in their upper body and head, this connectedness with the ground can be uncomfortable at first. Such people need to learn that the "airborne" quality that they had in their fragmented placement will now rise up from below their feet and the bottom of their torso, and permeate their whole body. Because of the upward and downward current of gravity, we are both rooted and flying at the same time.

The balance that occurs as we open to gravity involves the entire inner content and spectrum of our being. We are more balanced physically, our energy circulates more evenly, the functions of the two hemispheres of our brain are more balanced and integrated, and our attunement to fundamental consciousness becomes more symmetrical.

EXERCISE 14 *Balancing Attunement to Fundamental Consciousness*

Fundamental consciousness itself is always balanced. That is why it is motionless. Here is an exercise to help you balance your attunement to the dimension of fundamental consciousness. It is not helpful to try to hold your consciousness in a balanced position. But an exercise in balance will help you relax and settle into a more balanced attunement than before.

Mentally locate the space to the right of you.
Mentally locate the space to the left of you.

Now mentally locate the space to the right and the left of you at the same time.

Mentally locate the space in front of you.

Mentally locate the space behind you.

Now mentally locate the space in front and behind you at the same time.

You may notice that when you balance your attunement to space, you automatically arrive in the vertical core of your body. To be balanced is also to be centered.

Health and Healing

Although the body is always transformed by our realization of fundamental consciousness, we do not need a perfect physical body in order to become enlightened. A body that is disabled or ill can also be pervaded by fundamental consciousness. It is also said that certain rare spiritual masters have been able to keep their body intact through thousands of years. It seems likely that complete enlightenment does result in complete mastery and perfection of the physical body if one desires it. But this goal is in the extreme distant future. Even very advanced masters are seen to succumb to sickness, old age, and death. We can go a long way, however, to realizing fundamental consciousness in a body that is not perfect. Our defenses against life are mental at root. Anyone can release these defenses, regardless of their physical condition.

Although the realization of fundamental consciousness does not necessarily eliminate disablement or severe illness, it does offer some effective, subtle ways of healing the body. Subtle healing methods almost always take longer than conventional medicine, but they can sometimes heal what other approaches cannot. Subtle healing methods also effect a transformation of all levels of our being, so that our illness or injury becomes a path towards deeper enlightenment.

We can think, as Oriental medicine does, of all illness and injury as a reflection of blockages in our energy system. If we attune to fundamental consciousness in the area that is blocked, energy will begin to flow there again. One way to do this is as follows.

EXERCISE 15   *Subtle Healing*

15A) Mentally locate the center of your head.

From the center of your head, mentally find the area of your body that is ill or injured. If there is a particular area of pain or numbness, focus into the center of this area. You are finding the area of illness from the center of your head so that you can attune to the dimension of fundamental consciousness in that area. This is not a visualization exercise. Try to actually experience yourself in the center of your head and the area of illness.

Hold your attention steady in the center of your head and in the area of illness, and breathe smoothly and evenly through your nose.

15B) Another subtle healing method is through the use of balance. For example, if you are feeling pain in the left side of your jaw, mentally find the left and right sides of your jaw at the same time—balance your awareness of both sides of your jaw. As I said earlier, fundamental consciousness is the dimension of balance.

Both parts of the above exercise help contact the dimension of our being that is beyond our illness or injury. Fundamental consciousness is our uncontracted self. In this dimension there is no tension, and therefore no pain. When we contact fundamental consciousness in a particular part of the body, it has a (gradual) balancing effect on our energy and physical anatomy in that area.

Except in the case of mild, recent injury or tension, this type of healing usually requires repeated, consistent practice over time to be effective. In the case of illness, it can and should be combined with more immediate healing methods. We often become ill or injured in exactly the area of our being that we most need to awaken for our wholeness. To begin to gain consciousness and energy flow in an ill or disabled area is thus important for our personal growth, even if we are not able to entirely alleviate our physical condition.

Sensation

In our culture, most of us live more in the upper part of our body than in our pelvis and legs. In this fragmented consciousness, we can experience some awareness and love, but not very much physical sensation. For this reason, when many people speak of being "in the body," they are really referring to the regaining of the capacity for sensation. Without the aspect of physical sensation, we cannot experience either our oneness with the universe, or our wholeness within our self.

It is often our sensation and sexuality that are wounded and repressed in childhood. Any situation that prohibits or unduly limits our vitality, budding sexuality, or power will effect our level of physical sensation by causing us to constrict the bottom third of our body. Typically, cultural and religious taboos against sexual feelings are transmitted to children by sexually repressed adults. There is also widespread sexual abuse of children by adults, either overt or more subtly intrusive, that leaves children with deep-rooted trauma and defense in their capacity for sensation. As I write, we are experiencing a backlash against the attention that has been paid to this subject in recent years. But based on my years of clinical experience, I firmly believe that the problem of denial of sexual abuse still outweighs the problems of false memory and therapeutic malpractice.

The diminished physical sensation that so many people ex-perience is also a legacy of the religions of the last two thousand years, particularly in the West, which emphasized the transcendent nature of spiritual experience, and focused on the cultivation of love and awareness. This religious focus mirrored the Western culture's general alienation from the body and from nature, its ignorance and belittlement of nature's patterns, purposes, and underlying consciousness. The sensation aspect of fundamental consciousness is a quality most familiar to shamanistic and ancient goddess religions, which also emphasized the immanence of spirit within the forms present in nature.

The realization of the sensation aspect heals not only our own spiritual fragmentation, but also the schism which has existed in spiritual philosophy. As we become whole, we realize that there is no conflict between the transcendence and monotheism of the male sky-god religions and the immanence of the female, polytheistic, nature-oriented religions. Spiritual maturity is the realization of a dimension that is both immanent and transcendent at the same time, and which contains as an inseparable unity the aspects of awareness, love, and physical sensation.

Movement

The transformation of the body naturally transforms the way we move. Instead of moving with only the superficial muscle structure, we experience that we are moving through the whole inner depth of our body, with all the dimensions of our being—physical matter, energy, and fundamental consciousness. It is important that we practice moving through the dimension of fundamental consciousness so that we can move through the activities of our life without losing our spiritual realization. This is not just a practice of being mindful of our movements, but of moving with our fundamental mind.

EXERCISE 16 *Moving through Fundamental Consciousness*

16A) Here is one exercise to access and move through fundamental consciousness in your wrists.

Sit in a chair or cross-legged on a pillow. Rest your hands on your legs, with the palms down.

Mentally find the center of your head, between your ears, and between your face and the back of your head.

From the center of your head, find the inside of both wrists.

Balance your awareness of the inside of both wrists—find the inside of both wrists at the same time.

Staying in the center of your head, and the inside of both wrists, slowly lift your hands, palms down, towards your chest. Match the quality inside your wrists to the quality inside the center of your head as you move.

Staying inside the center of your head and inside both wrists, slowly turn your hands palm up and bring them back down towards your legs.

16B) Here is an exercise to access and move through fundamental consciousness inside your arms. You can practice this exercise sitting, standing, or lying on your back.

Bring your arms straight out to the side, perpendicular to your torso.

Feel that you are inside your shoulder sockets, arms, wrists, and hands. Feel that you inhabit your arms completely, from the shoulder sockets to the fingertips. Feel the quality of your self inside your arms, a particular quality that feels like your self.

Slowly bring your hands towards each other so that your arms make a circle in front of your chest. As you move, stay within the internal space of your hands and arms, and within the sense of your self. It should feel as if you are moving cell by cell. There are no gaps in the movement. It feels as if the inner space of the arms is moving through the space of the room.

Now open your arms back out to the side, staying inside your arms and hands.

Conclusion

To be attuned to fundamental consciousness throughout our whole body means that we embody the essence of our being. We experience that we exist as an individual form, that we take up space, and that our being has substance and depth. As fundamental conscious-ness pervading our body, we possess the qualities of understanding, voice, love, power, sexuality, and gender.

This self-possession always produces a shift in the way we feel about ourselves. It is impossible for us to hate ourselves, for example, if we experience that love dwells naturally in our body. It is impossible to feel overwhelmed by the environment when we experience power within our body. Self-possession also affects how we treat our body with regard to food, sexual relationships, rest, air, and other environmental conditions.

As our realization continues to deepen, we are able to inhabit more of the inner space of our body. It feels as if our individual form is being born. From the inner space of our own body, we are able to attune to the inner space of the bodies of other people. We feel a resonance between the essential qualities within our body and theirs. We begin to experience a full body relationship with all the other forms of life around us.

6

Person and Cosmos

The whole universe is of one and the same root as my
own self, and all things are one with me.

— Seng Chao

WE HAVE SEEN how fundamental consciousness is the basis of our
individual wholeness, and the basis of our oneness with other
people. It is also the basis of an even more mysterious experience:
our sense of oneness with the universe. This oneness is beyond the
awe, devotion, or ecstasy we may feel for the grandeur and vastness
of the firmament. It is a felt sense that we are continuous and unified
with the cosmos—that our own awareness, love, and sensation are
the vast awareness, love, and sensation of the universe.

Many spiritual teachings refer to the oneness of the individual
and the universe. The Tibetan Buddhist teacher Namkhai Norbu
writes, "When one realizes oneself, one realizes the essential nature
of the universe. The existence of duality is only an illusion and when
the illusion is undone, the primordial unity of one's own nature and
the nature of the universe is realized, or made real."

My perspective, as I've emphasized throughout this book, is that
the illusion of duality is not undone, but completed. As separate
individuals, we are in a process of completing ourselves as discrete

wholes *at the same time* that we are in a process of becoming (or
realizing that we are) entirely unified with the cosmos. In practical
terms, this means that for the long duration of our growth towards
complete enlightenment, the experience of I and other is actually
becoming clearer, more real. Our sense of relationship and dialogue
with other people as well as with the vast consciousness of the
universe becomes less veiled by projection and defense, allowing
for greater contact and intimacy.

We are always unified with the cosmos in the dimension of fundamental consciousness, even before we realize it. Many people
have experienced, through intense prayer or concentration, a sense
of relationship with the cosmos, and have received answers to their
questions and solutions to their problems. But when we begin to
realize fundamental consciousness, this connection and communion
become ongoing aspects of our lives.

We feel an increasing sense of love for the universe, and we feel
loved by the universe. This is an experience of relationship, or
duality. But at the same time, we experience that the love pervading
the universe is the same love that flows from our own heart. We are
engaged in an exchange of love with that which is fundamentally
our own self. This is what I mean by the experiences of duality
and oneness occurring, and developing, simultaneously.

In the same way, we have a clearer sense of response from the
universe when we call on it with our questions and problems. But at
the same time, we are beginning to experience that the wisdom and
creativity of the universe is our own wisdom and creativity. To call on
the universe (on God) is exactly the same as calling on our own mind.

The basic oneness of person and cosmos in the dimension of fundamental consciousness creates the phenomenon of synchronicity.
Synchronicity is the congruence between our inner psychological
process and the outer circumstances of our life. For example, we
may need to ask a friend a question, and run into her on our way
to work. Or, on another level, we may be working on feeling less

intimidated by other people, and a situation arises at work in which it is necessary for us to confront our boss. People who observe their lives carefully realize that these synchronistic events occur too frequently to be viewed as simple coincidence.

It is evident, from the existence of synchronicity, that the lives of all beings are coordinated in the unified field of fundamental consciousness. We can view the universe as a system in which all of the parts are engaged in a process of mutual integration (the realization of oneness) and expansion. In Buddhism, this process is called *pratitya samutpada*—the interdependent co-arising of all phenomena. Each part of this system arises from, and is pervaded by, one consciousness, one root. We can view each individual as an open "sub-system" within the larger system of the universe. The universe and the individual are mutually involved in the individual's process towards complete individuation and total union with the universe.

I will discuss three ways in which the universe is involved in our becoming enlightened—through stimulation, response to our desires, and gravity.

Stimulation

The infant is born with the potential for intelligence, love, power and sexuality. But we know that this potential will not develop without a mother's or primary caretaker's love and attention. A neglected infant suffers psychological and developmental deficits and may even die from lack of nurture. Thus, from the very beginning of life, we are dependent upon the environment to awaken our most basic capacities. As Daniel N. Stern documents, we grow in our self-knowledge and our ability to communicate with others within the matrix of the child-parent relationship.

There are two components to the stimulation of the environment on the growing child. One component is the realm of education. The child develops her capacities as she learns the world around her. She imitates other people and is faced with a variety of challenges that elicit new levels of functioning and integration. The other component is more subtle, but just as crucial for the child's growth. This component can be called "direct transmission," a term that is used to describe the expansion of consciousness that occurs for spiritual students in the presence of the teacher's expanded consciousness; this is a process of vibratory resonance. In the same way, the parent's love stimulates and deepens the child's capacity for love. The parent's awareness stimulates the child's awareness. And the parent's physical sensation stimulates the child's sensation.

The child's openness is also transmitted to the parents. But the impressionable child is much more formed by the parents than the other way around. As I have already described, the child has not yet individuated towards her core at all. She is in a state of relative undifferentiation from her environment, which is very different from the oneness of fundamental consciousness accessed in the core. Although the undefended child loves without inhibition, she does not love with the intensity or depth of an adult. Likewise, her capacity for awareness and sensation, although unfettered, are still in a rudimentary state.

Just as the child must inevitably learn a somewhat skewed knowledge of the world from her somewhat imperfect parents, she will also be unevenly stimulated by her parents' transmission of their own pattern of openness and defense. For example, a mother who is very loving but sexually repressed will be able to stimulate her child's love, but not her child's sensation. Of course, in addition to this automatic transmission of our parents' limitations, we are also making our own defenses against the painful circumstances in our environment. So, as we are awakening to life, we are also closing off to life. The parts of ourselves that we close off will not be available for stimulation from the environment.

As we continue to mature, other influences come into our lives and contribute to our growth. In the expanded environment of school and other activities, we continue to learn about ourselves and the world, and we continue to be awakened by the awareness, love, and sensation of the life around us.

The awareness, love, and sensation that make up the fundamental consciousness of the universe stimulate and awaken the potentials of our being in the same way as the other people in our environment. The vast consciousness of the universe is like a great spiritual master in whose presence we are always living. This consciousness, pervading all creation, is transmitted to us through nature and is also always present within ourselves as our most subtle dimension of consciousness. Throughout our lifetime, we constantly receive the "direct transmission" of enlightenment from the fundamental consciousness of the universe.

Desire and Response

Another way in which the universe matures us is by providing us with circumstances that release and resolve our bound pain. There is a great dichotomy in metaphysical thought about the relationship of the individual to his circumstances. One school sees us as helpless servants to an almighty deity, and counsels us to receive humbly and gratefully all that comes our way. Although we may petition the deity to lighten our burden, we are expected to have faith that there is complete wisdom and purpose even in our misfortunes, and we are expected to surrender our own small will to the will of God. We are expected to receive life just as it is given. The other school says that we ourselves are the creators of our circumstances. Even our most painful situations occur because we desire and will them. And by focusing intently on a visualization of our desired future, we can consciously create the life of our own choice.

Although these two philosophies seem incompatible on the surface, I believe that they are both essentially true. The desires that create our circumstances are, for the most part, the old unfulfilled desires of our childhood that are buried out of our conscious reach in our body. Our will is surrendered to the unfolding of this buried content as it creates the circumstances that are necessary for its resolution and release.

The careful observer sees that the contents of our bound childhood pain emerge into the arena of daily life in order for bound emotions to be expressed and unmet needs fulfilled. For example, I worked with a woman whose greatest childhood wounds were the sudden death of her father when she was seven, followed by the sudden death of her mother when she was sixteen. She came to me because the fatal heart attack of her husband several years before had left her so shattered that she was still unable to function at work or as a mother. His death had left her with the same bleak despair and sense of utter helplessness that she had felt as a child at the death of her parents. In order to overcome this crisis, she had to complete the mourning process for her parents that she had been too alone and afraid to experience as a child. She also had to develop enough self-possession to be able to tolerate the loss of love and support from the people she had most depended upon. She had to acknowledge and express the conflicted emotions of grief and anger at this loss, and the guilt she felt at surviving and going on with her life.

Many psychological theorists have remarked on the correspondences between our psychological history and our circumstances. Sigmund Freud was fascinated by our tendency to find ourselves in the same painful circumstance repeatedly. He called this phenomenon "repetition compulsion" and described it as "the manifestation of the power of the repressed." He based psychoanalysis on the client's compulsion to project his painful relationship with his parents onto the therapist, thus repeating, or attempting to repeat, the painful circumstances of his childhood in the therapist's office. Arnold Mindell's Process Therapy describes a similar notion that the client will "dream up" the therapist, actually influencing him to behave in ways that resemble his parents' behavior towards him in his childhood. Harville Hendrix claims that we choose our mate based on our unresolved childhood needs. He suggests that what he calls the "old brain" holds our painful childhood memories and watches for a potential mate with the familiar attributes of our parents.

Although most theorists explain the correspondence between childhood pain and adult circumstances as the result of subconscious attraction and choice, it is clear from the intimate details we learn of our client's lives over the years that many situations do not fit into this category. It is interesting to read Freud's struggle to remain "rational" in the evidence of his own observations. He writes, "We are more impressed by the cases where the subject appears to have a passive experience, over which he has no influence, but in which he meets with a repetition of the same fatality." On the following page he offers a somewhat qualified contradiction of this statement: "A great deal of what might be described as the compulsion of destiny seems intelligible on a rational basis; so that we are under no necessity to call in a new and mysterious motive force to explain it."

Freud did not seem to view the repetition compulsion as a part of a natural healing process, that goes on in life regardless of the intervention of a therapist, but rather as a symptom of neurosis. But I suggest that it is, along with other "manifestations of the power of the repressed." Many people who observe their growth process carefully report that as they come to a new area of work on themselves, events in their life emerge to bring them the means to facilitate this work. An illustration of this was a woman who, as a child, had been repeatedly told to be quiet and not disturb the adults with her "silly chatter." When I first met her she was very subdued and spoke almost in a whisper. Shortly after I began working with her, one of her massage clients was unable to pay for his sessions and suggested that she do a trade with him. It turned out that he taught singing classes, and specialized in healing psychological blocks to vocal expression. Around the same time, she was looking for work as a dance therapist, with little success. Just as she was ready to give up, a job became available at a nursing home for a music therapist. Although she had no experience as a music therapist, the home's director offered her the job. As a music therapist she was required, almost daily, to lead the nursing home residents in song. This activity, along with the singing lessons, helped loosen the tension that she had held in her throat for so many years. She was able to express herself much more easily, and her voice became strong and confident.

As I have said, the pervasive, unified intelligence of fundamental consciousness is the basis of synchronicity. Here we see that synchronicity is part of the healing function of the universe. The correspondences between inner and outer experience are not random. They reflect the partnership between our fragmented incomplete self and the intelligence of our wholeness in a natural process of unfolding towards total unity.

I am suggesting that the universe responds to the desires and needs of our childhood mentality buried in our body. The universe also responds to our conscious desires, if we focus our will with enough intensity. This accounts for the efficacy of prayer and visualization. However, our conscious desires are often in conflict with our unconscious desires, and this diminishes our creative power. It seems that the universe continues to respond to our unconscious desires until they are made conscious and resolved.

I worked with a woman whose greatest desire was to get married. She made a daily practice of visualizing herself meeting the right man and happily settling down with him. Although she approached this practice with determination, she often found it difficult to get a clear image of herself as happily married. She finally realized that she had an old image of married life that entirely contradicted this happy picture. The old image was based on her mother, married to an alcoholic and the mother of four children, crying and threatening to leave, and then crying even more bitterly because she felt she never could leave. The fear of being trapped in an intolerable situation like that of her mother kept her from wholeheartedly visualizing herself married.

Recently the view that our circumstances are the result of our desires has come under fire from people dealing with severe illness. They say that this philosophy makes them feel ashamed of becoming ill, as if their illness showed some lack of willpower. It must be recognized that the causes of illness, and most likely other circumstances as well, are complex. The immune system is weakened not only by our psychological state but by pollution, viruses, and so on. The metaphysical causes are themselves complex and difficult to analyze. However, to the extent that illness is caused by psychological conditions, it is not usually the present emotional or mental state that is responsible. Emotional pain, when held in the body for decades, can cause severe blockages in our energy circulation. It is this blockage that eventually causes illness. This is in no way a sign of weakness on the part of the sufferer. No one is entirely without bound childhood pain in their body. But it does mean that there is the possibility of healing through the release of these psychological holding patterns. Besides healing through the release of bound emotional pain, some people have been able to heal themselves through visualization and prayer, and through the subtle attunement described in the previous chapter. This potential is very real and should not be disregarded because it is not always successful.

We create our lives in partnership with the wisdom of our wholeness. Although we can use our creative power to influence our lives, we must also surrender to the spontaneous aspect of our growth process. As incomplete individuals there is much we don't know about the nature of death or the possibility of rebirth, and we cannot be totally sure what the most positive outcome is for ourselves in the long run. Tibetan Buddhism teaches that the practice of visualization should always end with dissolving the image into empty consciousness. The release of the visualization is as important for its effectiveness as the visualization itself. We grow by a combination of creativity and surrender, will and spontaneity.

The desire/response aspect of our relationship with the universe is often dismissed as the worst sort of New Age babble. It can easily be labeled "magical thinking," one of psychology's worst insults, because it does point to a magical aspect of nature. But this is a magic that goes on all the time in our lives and is one of the basic laws of the universe. Hindu metaphysics calls the universe a "wish-fulfilling gem." In recent years the Indian doctor Deepak Chopra has brought this idea to a growing Western audience by referring to the "cosmic computer" that we can connect with in order to "achieve the spontaneous fulfillment of desires."

Earlier in this book I said that the individual is like a twist or coil in the fabric of fundamental consciousness. The individual is trying to untwist, to regain his essential oneness with fundamental consciousness. And fundamental consciousness is trying to rid itself of this twist in itself. The individual and the wholeness of fundamental consciousness are in partnership in this untwisting because they are basically the same consciousness. If we view the person/cosmos relationship as a system, we can also say that this system is propelled by entropy—the tendency of all systems towards the equilibrium that is their undoing. In other words, the twist that is our incomplete self tends to untwist, tends towards the balance and oneness that will ultimately be the extinction of the system. (Complete enlightenment is often called extinction, or the "great death" in Buddhist terminology.)

The person/cosmos system is propelled towards equilibrium through stimulation, desire/response, and (as we will see in the next section) gravity. Desire arises out of the tension of our incompleteness, of our twisting away from reality. We project our desire onto material possessions, etc., but all desire is basically the desire to be free from the tension of our incompleteness. Desire is the force of our will towards equilibrium and wholeness. All fulfillment of desire is experienced as pleasure because it releases tension.

It is important to be carefully attuned to our desires for they form our individual path towards wholeness. As Joseph Campbell put it, we should "follow our bliss." As the unconscious desires of our bound childhood mentality become resolved, our circumstances begin to match our conscious desires. We become less fragmented, and our desire also becomes less fragmented. We begin to experience that we desire wholeness, that we crave connection with our self and others, that we want to penetrate through the numb parts of ourselves to awaken our total consciousness. At this point, the universe, our own completed self, provides us with opportunities to work directly on our maturity.

Gravity

Perfect balance is complete enlightenment. Balance is our alignment with Earth's gravitational field; it is our oneness, our true relationship with the Earth. As I said in the previous chapter, gravity moves not on us but through us, because we are not solid objects but open vibrational fields. As we release our defensive grip on our self, as we settle the weight of our whole being to the ground, a force rises upward from the Earth, through the space of our body, energy, and mind, and pulls us towards balance. Wherever we have closed our organism against life's stimulation, we are out of balance. The movement of gravity pushes against these defensive skews, like water pushing against a barrier. It is as if we are each learning to ride Earth's movement through space, without interference. As we become more open to gravity, we become more balanced. Openness, balance, and enlightenment are synonymous. Therefore the Earth's (and our own) movement through space are directly involved in our process of maturing.

It is the force of our movement through space that moves through our body, penetrating our body with increasing depth as we become more open. I think it is worth considering that the powerful energy that finally moves through the vertical core of our body (*kundalini*) in the advanced stages of our opening is this same force of our movement through space. Since we realize fundamental consciousness through the vertical core of our body, this advanced stage in our alignment with gravity corresponds to our realization of fundamental consciousness.

The essential role of gravity in our process of enlightenment makes relaxation an important part of spiritual practice. For gravity to penetrate inward in our body, we need to surrender to it, we need to rest. This also shows the importance of sleep for our natural growth process. In sleep, our body is at its most relaxed. This may explain why there is often spontaneous emergence and resolution of our bound pain in our dreams. Just as the stimulation of the universe and our life circumstances bring our bound pain to consciousness, the movement of gravity through our body also penetrates our bound pain and brings it to consciousness.

Spontaneity

In chapter 3, I divided our growth process into two components—healing and realization. Both these components are spontaneous. Our relationship with the universe awakens the subtle potentials of our being, at the same time as it facilitates the movement of our bound pain towards consciousness. In psychotherapy we work on the healing component of our growth and in spiritual disciplines we work on the realization component. Although we can make this division in theory, in practice the two modalities are inextricably related. As we heal psychologically, we have more access to our fundamental consciousness, and as we realize fundamental consciousness we can more easily release our psychological pain. But in both the psychotherapeutic and spiritual modalities, we are only facilitating a process that is spontaneous and inherent in our nature.

Many schools of psychological and spiritual thought are recognizing the spontaneity of the growth process. Rebirthing and EMDR (Eye Movement Desensitization and Reprocessing therapy) for example, are ways to facilitate the natural unwinding of the knotted skein of our holding patterns. In general, a new understanding is dawning in psychotherapy that cautions the therapist to follow the lead of the client's process as she presents it in the session, rather than approach her with a static diagnosis and treatment plan.

Zen Buddhism teaches a meditation called *shikan-taza* which is the practice of sitting still without any particular object of concentration. It is taught that just sitting still and breathing will gradually unfold the meditator towards enlightenment. The Zen teacher and scholar Philip Kapleau writes, "The very foundation of shikan-taza is an unshakable faith that sitting as the Buddha sat, with the mind void of all conceptions, of all beliefs and points of view, is the actualization or unfoldment of the inherently enlightened Bodhi-mind with which all are endowed."

The Dzog-chen school of Tibetan Buddhism teaches the same technique of sitting still as the mind gradually clears and realizes fundamental consciousness. The Tibetan Buddhist teacher Chogyam Trungpa Rinpoche wrote, "one can free oneself like a snake unwinding."

The imagery of unwinding is often used to describe the nature of personal growth. Christian parlance refers to our human coil, or our coil of suffering. I am suggesting that the bound pain in our body really is a coil, a twisting away from life. And each pocket of buried memory and pain contains the tension of that twist. As in archery, when the bow is pulled taut to release the arrow, the held tensions in our body also contain the momentum for their return to their origin, once the process of release has begun. This momentum, released through stimulation, desire/response, and the movement of gravity, produces the spontaneous unfolding of the healing com-ponent of our path towards wholeness.

Projections onto God

We begin to experience our oneness with the universe, and our advanced phase of individuation, as we access the vertical core of our body. With this development, we begin to realize that our primary environment is not society, but the cosmos itself. This does not in any way undermine our sense of social integrity or our enjoyment in the company of human beings. In fact we are able to interact with the world with increased clarity and appreciation. But our sense of belonging in the world is integrated with a sense of belonging to something beyond, and in some sense more real, than the world around us. Also, our ambition to succeed in the world is tempered by the new understanding that our primary goal does not rely on worldly success. We are attuned to a dimension that is not affected by the opinions and fashions of our society. In becoming our authentic self, we become original. We are using our own senses to perceive the world and our own cognitive abilities to understand and respond to the world. At this point, I believe, we are of far greater value to our society.

We also receive love and sustenance from our relationship with the universe. This means that we no longer need to be "mirrored" by another human being in order to feel that we exist, or that we have value. We do not need to share an experience with someone in order to fully experience it ourselves. Although we are capable of more pleasure and intimacy with others than ever before, we do not need to be in relationship with someone in order to feel loved. Love and existence are constant, natural qualities of fundamental consciousness and of our oneness with the cosmos. To the extent that we have realized fundamental consciousness, we no longer feel the "existential" anxiety of aloneness.

As we realize fundamental consciousness, we release our loyalty to the constricting patterns of our relationship with our childhood family. We gradually see through the projections that we have made of our childhood family onto our present relationships. And we find that we must undergo the same process in our relationship with the universe.

Most of us have been forming since childhood some (usually

unconscious) notion of the source of fortune and misfortune, some image of God that now obscures our direct relationship with the universe. God is often presented to children in the guise of a distant parental figure, with the power to punish and reward. In fact, much of Western religion imagines God in this form. This image locks us into an attitude of servitude and reverence that keeps us from knowing our own essential self as ultimate reality. People in this relationship with God consider the realization of the self as God to be sacrilege and *hubris*. Certainly it is the worst affront to the authority of the parental image of God. But if we do not know that our own self is ultimate reality, we will not experience the true one-ness that underlies and pervades all life. For we can only enter into this oneness by subtle attunement to our own self.

We easily project onto a parental figure of God the imperfect, conditional love that we received from our parents. For example, I worked with a man who had a deep-rooted sense of not belonging, of being rejected by God. He could not imagine good things happening to him, because he knew that God did not want him to be happy. He was resistant to experiencing fundamental consciousness pervade his body, because he did not want to try to feel connected to something that had rejected him. As I got to know him better, I learned that he had been sent away to live at a boarding school when he was three years old, for the duration of his childhood, even though both his parents were alive. He had never, even as a child, allowed himself to feel his pain and confusion at this rejection, but instead directed his sense of alienation towards God.

Most religious teaching implies that we must beg God for our well-being and good fortune. At worst, we are taught that God does not want us to be whole, that he frowns on sexuality, self-expression, and self-love. I worked with a woman who told me that she had rebelled against God in order to be herself. Unfortunately, she paid a high price for this rebellion. Although she felt independent, she was unable to feel like a good person because she felt in conflict with God. She presented a flamboyant "bad" persona that masked a deeper sense of shame and self-loathing. Even more troubling for her was a sense of being cut off from God, from her true relationship with the universe and her deep spiritual self. But she was convinced that to feel this connection, she would have to give up her sexuality and her right to think for herself. As she began to examine her life history, however, she realized that it was in her childhood home and her Sunday school classes that her sensual vitality and her developing opinions were rejected.

We also make positive projections onto the universe, for example imagining it as the Mother or the all-forgiving Jesus. These projections can be helpful at points in our development because they accurately portray the attributes of the cosmic intelligence, and provide useful metaphors for our relationship with the cosmos. But even these images must eventually be dropped for us to have direct contact and oneness with the cosmos. There is a story that the great Hindu teacher Ramakrishna used to worship a stone carving of Krishna. One day Ramakrishna dreamed that his own teacher appeared to him and rubbed the stone against his forehead until he was in great pain and resolved to give up this dualistic spiritual practice.

As we let go of our projections, we begin to experience the perfect love and benevolence of the universe, of our own completed self. We are able to receive its nurture and rely on its laws of evolution. This means that we no longer have to hold ourselves rigidly separate and alone in a desperate attempt to survive either the unpredictable whims of a distant god or the random calamities of a godless universe. We can surrender to the natural unfolding of events in our life, and to the pervasive awareness, love, and sensation that unifies us with the vast consciousness of the cosmos. As Karlfried Graf Durckheim writes, "Faith is innate in every man thanks to the bond which unites him with the ground of Being." The faith that so many of us have lost in our conflict with the God of our childhood, returns with the realization of fundamental consciousness, not just as belief, but as an innate quality of our being.

I have found that many psychological problems that do not seem affected by our awareness of their childhood origin will finally heal when we experience our relationship with the universe. One woman came to me because she had been eating compulsively all her life. She was able to uncover the source of her problem: that she had substituted food for her mother's ambivalent love, but continued to eat far beyond her physical hunger. She was terrified that the feeling of not being loved would destroy her if she did not keep filling her emotional emptiness with food. It was not until she realized fundamental consciousness, and could actually feel the love of the universe pervading her inside and out, that she was able to give up the excess food. Similarly, I worked with a man who kept saying, "I know I wasn't loved as a child but what should I do about it? There's just something missing in me." In fact, there is nothing missing in us, no matter what our childhood experience was. But because of our early pain, we defend against the love that is inside and all around us. When we can release this resistance and allow ourselves to experience our oneness with the cosmos, we feel love as a constant aspect of our being.

Dharma—the Ethics of Fundamental Consciousness

Our true relationship with the universe contains an inherent ethical perspective. As we realize that our own essential being is a dimension of consciousness that is also the essential being of all other life, we feel an underlying kinship with everyone we meet. We can use the metaphor of a musical instrument. If we are all basically pianos, even if we meet a piano playing a tune quite different than our own, we can feel in our being the potential to play his tune also. When we know our self as the pervasive ground of life, we have learned the basic language of all beings, including animals and plants. In this shared field of fundamental consciousness, we do not need to adopt a static attitude of goodwill that obscures the richness of our feelings and the directness of our contact with our self and others. To actually experience the heart of a bird, or the subtle awareness of a tree, or the complex emotions in another person, evokes a spontaneous response of empathy and compassion.

There is also a more subtle manifestation of ethics in fundamental consciousness. This is expressed in the Sanskrit word *dharma*. In Buddhist tradition, this word has several connotations. It means the Buddhist metaphysical understanding of the universe and enlightenment, the teaching of this understanding, and the living of this understanding. The direct translation of "dharma" is "justice." To live dharmically is to practice the justice of enlightenment. But this practice is not a preconceived set of behaviors. It is the alignment of oneself with the metaphysical laws of the universe and the great benevolence inherent in those laws. To the extent that we have realized fundamental consciousness, we are unified with the wisdom and love of the whole, and with the spontaneous unwinding towards enlightenment of all forms in creation. In this dimension, our own choices of action are the choices of the universe, and all our actions serve the progression towards enlightenment of all life, including our own. We do not have to shame ourselves into doing good works. Our own truth will benefit the truth of the life around us.

The idea that we can be aligned with the will of God also exists in Western religion. In Judaism, there is the concept of the *mitzvah*, which has a range of meaning from a good deed to a general attitude of justness and benevolence towards others. Jewish scholar Abraham J. Heschel writes, "Every act done in agreement with the will of God is a mitzvah." Hassidic writer Reb Zalman Schachter defines mitzvah as "the divine will doing itself through the vehicle of the now egoless devotee."

Christian interpreter Maurice Nicoll writes, "When Good comes first, a man acts from mercy and grace. Then he is made Whole. When he is Whole, he no longer misses the mark." In this quote we have the idea that the individual becomes whole by being good. And we have the more subtle idea, very similar to the Buddhist idea of dharma, that he is now right on target, that he does not "miss the mark." That mark is the action that benefits everyone involved.

Conclusion

Above all else, the spiritual path is a process of becoming real. Our true nature is wholeness within our self and unity with the cosmos. To proceed on the spiritual path, we need to embrace this paradox: We grow towards completeness as separate individuals at the same time as we transcend our separateness and become one with the cosmos. Both involve the unfolding of our essential human qualities—awareness, love, and sensation. Both require the integration of love and detachment, distance and intimacy.

We cannot become real by pretending to be other than who we are right now. Even after we have begun our realization of fundamental consciousness, we are still incomplete, fragmented people, at the same time as we are attuned to the dimension of wholeness and unity. This means that we retain our human right to sing the blues, even though we are increasingly capable of joy and peace.

As our realization progresses, our yearning for completeness grows stronger. Eventually it becomes central in our lives, the basis of our life choices, and the primary source of our satisfaction. In the modern world, as in probably all previous eras, the growing individual must swim against the powerful, hypnotic tides of ignorance and disbelief. When we realize fundamental consciousness, we live in a dimension that is unknown to most people. We then have only our own perception to guide and reassure us. We must trust the subtle signs that mark our own personal path towards wholeness— the deepening currents of energy in our body, the freedom of our breath, the radiance in the air, the synchronicity between outer events and our inner hopes and needs, and the expansion of our consciousness pervading our body and environment. Although religious affiliation is certainly an option, once we have entered the dimension of fundamental consciousness, there is no necessity for outward ritual or excessive discipline. The path emerges as we go, bringing us the circumstances and practices to facilitate our growth. Since our contemporary world rarely supports us for shaving our heads or carrying a begging bowl, we must each find our own way to live and interact with the more conventional aspects of society, while remaining on our unique, invisible path. At the core of everyone and everything is the radiant, unbroken "I," the root of the universe. When we live in this core, we experience the natural integration of the body, the true self, and the transcendent, pervasive ground of fundamental consciousness.

Notes

CHAPTER ONE: *Defining Enlightenment*

2   Everything in the universe . . .: Seng Chao (374–414 A.D.), traditional Zen koan.

3   I am the supreme Brahman . . .: Sri Shankaracharya, *Upadesa Sahasri*, trans. Swami Jagadananda (Mylapore, India: Sri Ramakrishna Math Printing Press, 1989), 111.

CHAPTER TWO: *Defining Self and Selflessness*

21   let go of personal life . . .: Ken Wilber, *The Atman Project* (Wheaton, IL: The Theosophical Publishing House, 1980), 148.

22   Dalai Lama: There are two types of "I" . . .: John F. Avedon, *Interview with the Dalai Lama* (New York: Littlebird Publications, 1980), 63–64.

23   Psychologists such as Alice Miller . . .: Alice Miller, *The Drama of the Gifted Child*, trans. Ruth Ward (New York: Basic Books, 1981).

28   We have asserted the truth of substantiality . . .: A.H. Almaas, *Essence* (York Beach, ME: Samuel Weiser Inc., 1986), 76.

39   One experiences oneself as an emptiness . . .: A.H. Almaas, *The Pearl Beyond Price* (Berkeley, CA: Diamond Books, 1988), 427.

40   We have seen that the same reality . . .: Chandradhar Sharma, *A Critical Survey of Indian Philosophy* (Nagar, India: Motilal Banarsidass, Jawahar, 1987), 25.

41   center of gravity shifting . . .: Daniel N. Stern, *The Interpersonal World of the Infant* (New York: Basic Books, 1985), 209.

44 The old idea is that the personality . . .: A.H. Almaas, *Essence* (York Beach, ME: Samuel Weiser Inc., 1986), 59.

48 Know that which has form . . .: Ashtavakra, *Ashtavakra Samhita*, trans. Swami Nityaswarupananda (Calcutta, India: Advaita Ashrama, 1981), 14–15.

48 unifying subjective perspective . . .: Daniel N. Stern, *The Interpersonal World of the Infant* (New York: Basic Books, 1985)

CHAPTER THREE: *The Healing Process*

52 Do away with your superimposition . . .: Sri Shankaracharya, *Vivekacu-damani*, rendered by Judith Blackstone.

53 A baby does experience essence . . .: A.H. Almaas, *Essence* (York Beach, ME: Samuel Weiser Inc., 1986), 84.

58 character armor and muscular armor . . .; the result of a binding . . .; In armored human organisms . . .; I have also explained . . .; What remains puzzling . . .: Wilhelm Reich, *Character Analysis*, trans. Vincent R. Carfagno (New York: Touchstone, 1945), 352; 352; 372; 378; 378.

CHAPTER FOUR: *Distance and Intimacy*

72 In the fifties, Margaret Mahler formulated . . .: Margaret Mahler, *The Psychological Birth of the Human Infant* (New York: Bantam Books, 1975).

73 Attachment and separation . . .: Daniel N. Stern, *The First Relationship* (Cambridge, MA: Harvard Univ. Press, 1977), 128.

73 sense of emergent self . . .; acquisition of new senses . . .: Daniel N. Stern, *The Interpersonal World of the Infant* (New York: Basic Books, 1985), 10–11.

74 Female identity formation . . .: Carol Gilligan, *In a Different Voice* (Cambridge, MA: Harvard Univ. Press, 1982), 7–8; Nancy Chodorow, *The Reproduction of Mothering* (Berkeley, CA: University of California Press, 1978), 150,166–167; Robert J. Stoller, "A Contribution to the

Study of Gender Identity", *International Journal of Psycho-Analysis* 45 (1964): 220–226.

75   Clinical issues that . . .; look toward mother to read her face . . .: Daniel N. Stern, *The Interpersonal World of the Infant* (New York: Basic Books, 1985), 10; 132.

75   If the individual does not feel . . .: R.D. Laing, *The Divided Self* (Tavistock, 1959; Baltimore: Penguin, 1965), 52–53.

CHAPTER SIX: *Person and Cosmos*

116   The whole universe is of one and the same root . . .: Seng Chao (374– 414 A.D.), traditional Zen koan.

116   When one realizes oneself, . . .: Namkhai Norbu, *The Crystal and the Way of Light* (New York: Routledge & Kegan Paul, 1986), 124.

118   As Daniel N. Stern documents . . .: Daniel N. Stern, *The Interpersonal World of the Infant* (New York: Basic Books, 1985).

121   the manifestation of the power of the repressed: Sigmund Freud, *Beyond the Pleasure Principle*, trans. James Strachey (New York: W.W. Norton & Company, 1961), 14.

121   Harville Hendrix claims . . .: Harville Hendrix, *Getting the Love You Want* (New York: Harper Perennial, 1988), 9.

122   We are more impressed . . .: Sigmund Freud, *Beyond the Pleasure Principle*, trans. James Strachey (New York: W.W. Norton & Company, 1961), 16.

125   In recent years . . .: Leslie Miller quoting Deepak Chopra, article in *Marin Independent Journal*, July 10, 1994.

128   The very foundation of . . .: Philip Kapleau, *The Three Pillars of Zen* (Garden City, NY: Anchor Books, 1980), 7.

128   one can free oneself . . .: Chogyam Trungpa Rinpoche, *Mudra* (Berkeley, CA: Shambhala, 1972), 7.

131   Faith is innate in every man . . .: Karlfried Graf Durckheim, *Hara* (London: Unwin Hyman Limited, 1962), 11.

133   Every act done in agreement . . .: Abraham J. Heschel, *Between God and Man* (New York: The Free Press, 1959), 186.

133   the divine will doing itself . . .: Reb Zalman Schachter, *Fragments of a Future Scroll* (Germantown, PA: Leaves of Grass Press, 1975), 40.

133   When Good comes first, . . .: Maurice Nicoll, *The New Man* (New York: Penguin Books, 1967), 59.

Glossary

Causal Body: as described in the Hindu metaphysical system, one of the five sheaths (Sanskrit: *kosas*) of our being which conceal our fundamental dimension of consciousness. It is called the intelligence sheath (Sanskrit: *vijnanamayakosa*). It is responsible for both organizing the contraction in our being and releasing that contraction to become one with fundamental consciousness.

Chakras: sensitive points along the subtle core of the body and at other sites throughout our body where it is easiest to penetrate into the dimension of fundamental consciousness.

Dharma: the Sanskrit word for justice or righteousness. It is used in Buddhism to mean the nature of the universe, living and acting in accord with the nature of the universe, and the path of realizing the nature of the universe.

Direct Experience: when the perceiver and the perceived are unified in the all-pervasive field of fundamental consciousness, immediate and accurate perception which is no longer obstructed by psychological defense or preconception.

Energy System: the dynamic aspect of our being, formed by a complex circulatory system of vibrations, varying from gross to subtle, and moving through the vast stillness of fundamental consciousness.

Enlightenment: the realization—the lived experience—that the fundamental nature of our own being and everything else in nature is pure, unified, all-pervading consciousness; the ability to live in the dimension of fundamental consciousness, which pervades both one's individual body and everything in nature.

Essential Qualities: fundamental, experienced aspects of our being—such as sexuality, power, love, and intelligence—emanating from the vertical core of the body.

False Self: all of the defenses, static beliefs, and attitudes that conceal our fundamental dimension of consciousness.

Fundamental Consciousness: our most subtle, unified dimension of consciousness which pervades our individual body, the world, and the cosmos; the ultimate reality of everything in nature.

Individuation: the process of becoming fully oneself—a separate person with volition, feelings, perceptions, desires, and cognitions of one's own; the gradual penetration inward to the subtle core of the body which is the source of our essential qualities of being and our authentic sense of self.

Kundalini: the most subtle level of our energy system which runs through the vertical core of the body and a network of subtle channels branching out from this core.

Narcissism: the pretended inflation of one's sense of self in order to compensate for a hollow, diminished sense of self.

Non-Duality: the experienced unity, or continuity, of self and object in the dimension of fundamental consciousness.

Peak Experience: a momentary experience of intense impact, often accompanied by heightened sensory ability, insight, and vivid emotions such as awe or ecstasy.

Self-Realization: *see* Enlightenment.

Separation-Individuation Process: a psychological theory of early childhood development which describes a sequence of phases negotiating a gradual recognition of oneself as an individual person, separate from one's mother.

Subtle Nervous System: a complex system, charted in Hindu Yoga, of subtle channels, energy currents, and points (Sanskrit: *chakras*) throughout the body. The subtle nervous system's main channel is called *shushumna*, and runs through the vertical core of the body. Two more channels, known as *ida* and *pingala*, run on either side of shushumna, crossing at intervals to form a shape that resembles the double helix of DNA or the symbolic staff of the medical profession. The seven points along shushumna, where ida and pingala cross, are the main chakras of the body.

Subtle Self Work: a method developed by the author for realizing fundamental consciousness.

Synchronicity: the congruence between our inner psychological process and the outer circumstances of our life.

Vertical Core of the Body: a subtle channel in the central axis of the body which is our entranceway into the dimension of fundamental consciousness. It is called the central channel in Buddhism and shushumna in Hindu yoga. The more access we have to the vertical core of the body, the more space we gain in the dimension of fundamental consciousness.

Index

Index to the Exercises